Beginners' COMMUNICATION Games

Jill Hadfield

Longman

photocopiable material

Pearson Education Limited
Edinburgh Gate, Harlow
Essex CM20 2JE, England
and Associated Companies throughout the world.

www.longman.com

First published by Addison Wesley Longman Limited 1999
Sixth impression 2003
ISBN 0582 31891 2

Set in Plantin and Frutiger
Printed in China
NPCC/06

Produced for the Publishers by Sigma Associates
Designed by Christine Cox
Illustrated by: Maggie Brand (Maggie Mundy) (pp 47, 48, 54, 55, 65,
85, 86, 102, 103, 104); Phillip Burrows (pp 57, 58, 59, 77, 78, 89, 95);
Nicky Cooney (pp 61, 74, 76, 93); Christine Cox (p 63); Nigel Kitching
(pp 46, 49, 72, 73, 79, 80, 90, 96, 101); David Lock (pp 52, 53, 60, 66,
106-111); Liz Roberts (p 88); Francis Scappaticci (pp 67, 68, 69, 91, 92,
100); Ivana Svabic-Cannon (pp 62, 81, 97); TechType (maps) (pp 56, 87)

For

Peter Hill and Monica Vincent
who gave me so much help
when I was a beginner teacher

Foreword

This book wasn't my idea. *Elementary Communication Games* was published some years ago, and over the years I have had a number of requests for another book for beginners. At first, I resisted this idea - I thought 40 games was enough at elementary level - but as I listened to teachers in a variety of countries and different teaching situations, I understood that they meant not just another elementary book, but an elementary book with a difference. They wanted:

- a book at an even lower level, with very limited language, for almost total beginners
- games that were not too complex conceptually for beginners
- some support with the problem of how to set up and explain the games in language that beginners would understand
- games that were also suitable for younger learners

Well, I thought I'd have a go.

I have tried to meet these needs in the following ways:

1 Limitation of language

The language in *Beginners' Communication Games* is broken down into smaller chunks than in the previous book. There, several different exponents were often required for one game: here the language has been kept to one structure and one exchange, and a small number of new vocabulary items per game. For example, 'Looking for Mr X' in *Elementary Communication Games* requires the following: *What is his name? What is his address? What does he do? Where does he come from?* In *Beginners' Communication Games*, these structures are spread over five games which deal with names, numbers, addresses, jobs and nationality.

2 Conceptual complexity

I have tried to make the game structure in *Beginners' Communication Games* simpler. Some groups of beginners who are unfamiliar with communicative methods feel disorientated not only by the new language they have to absorb, but also by the new methods. I have tried to make the objective of the games as simple and easy to grasp as possible, and to build on game-types such as matching card games that students are likely to be familiar with from their home backgrounds. Each game has a clear and simple goal: only one operation is needed, e.g. match, find, collect, exchange, arrange or guess and, once these terms are understood by the students, it should be easy to demonstrate how to play. About a third of the games in the book are

pairwork, a third small group games, and a third whole class games. Teachers have sometimes found whole class games more difficult with beginners (probably because it is not so easy to monitor what is going on and find out who has not understood). I think it's important to include them for the sake of variety and also because they have a good effect on the dynamics of the group, encouraging students to mingle and giving them a sense of coming together as a group. But, mindful of teachers who find them more difficult to organise, I've designed most of these games so half the class can remain seated and only half get up and wander around. This will make it easier (a) for students to grasp the goal of the game and (b) for teachers to organise the game, particularly with large groups.

3 The problem of metalanguage

The problem with beginners is that any activity which entails more than *Do the exercise on page 15*, requires them to understand language which is far more complex than the tiny amount of language they have learned so far. This need not be seen as an insurmountable problem. In fact, it helps if you consider it in a positive light - and not as a problem at all: the explanations and instructions you will have to give to set up the games form a mini-listening comprehension course on their own! And the processes the students will go through - listening and watching as you explain and demonstrate, listening and doing as they carry out the instructions - form a very natural way of acquiring language, very similar to the processes a native speaker goes through when acquiring his/her own language.

I do recognise the problem though and have added new features in the Teacher's notes, which may be of special help to beginning teachers or teachers who are less familiar with communicative methods: (a) a step-by-step explanation of how to demonstrate how to play the game (through visual demonstrations rather than verbal explanations) together with (b) a list of the classroom language needed for setting up the game.

Another new feature is the provision of pictorial Rules sheets for the card games where roles are given in a strip cartoon form.

I hope that all these new features will make this book more suitable for beginners and slower learners.

4 Younger and older learners

I have tried to find a context for most games that is age-neutral (i.e. that avoids risqué topics and is neither ostensibly too adult nor too childish).

Contents

game	function	structures	topic area
1 Doppelganger	greetings and introductions	Hello. What's your name? My name is	names
2 Spelling lotto	spelling	——	letters of the alphabet
3 Ladybird bingo	numbers	——	numbers (1-20)
4 Clockmatch	telling the time	What's the time? It's	time
5 Lost in the post	asking for and giving personal information	What's your name? What's your address?	names and addresses
6 Wedding photos	asking and saying who someone is	Who's this/that? This is/That's X. He's/She's my	family members
7 Mine!	asking and saying who things belong to	Whose is this/are these? mine + possessives	family, clothes
8 National dress	asking about country and nationality	What's your name? My name is ... . Where are you from? I'm from/I'm	country and nationality
9 Don't worry!	asking about feelings	Are you ...? Yes, I am/No, I'm not. (Here you are.)	feelings
10 Identity parade	describing people	Is he/she ...? Yes, he/she is/No, he/she isn't.	people's appearances
11 Class colours	asking about preferences	What colour is/are ...?	colours
12 What is it?	describing objects/shapes	Is it ...? Yes, it is/No, it isn't.	size and shape
13 Happy Birthday	asking and saying when birthdays are	When is your birthday? It's in/on	numbers, months
14 Tools for the job	asking about jobs	What do you do?/What's your job? I'm a ... . Is this yours?	jobs
15 School photo	asking about jobs	What does X do now? He's/She's a	jobs
16 Packing	asking and saying where things are	Where's the ...? It's + prepositions of place	holidays and travel
17 Something old, something new	describing rooms	There is/isn't a ... . There are some/There aren't any	rooms and furniture
18 My home town	asking about town features	Is there a ...? Yes, there is/No, there isn't.	town features
19 Mother Hubbard	asking about existence and quantity	Is there any ...? How much is there? How many are there?	food and weights
20 Collectors	asking for things	Have you got ...? Yes, I have/No, I haven't.	kitchen objects

game	function	structures	topic area
21 The great shopping race	asking for things	Have you got any ...? Here you are. (How much/many do you want?)	shops and shopping
22 Martian lotto	describing appearances	Has he got ...? He's got/He hasn't got	people's appearances
23 Airport convention	describing appearances	He's/She's/They've got ... . He's/She's/They're	people's appearances and clothes
24 Follow the yellow brick road	giving directions	imperatives prepositions of movement and place	the countryside
25 Dream tickets	asking about likes and dislikes	Do you like -ing ...? Yes, I do/No, I don't. This is for you.	hobbies
26 Lost tribes	asking about habits and lifestyles	Do you ...? Yes, I do/No, I don't.	daily life
27 Does it eat people?	asking about habits	Does it ...? Yes, it does/No, it doesn't.	animals
28 Jobmatch	asking about daily routines	When do you ...? I ... at ... o'clock.	work routines
29 World map	asking about lifestyles	Where/What/How do you ...?	countries and customs
30 Lie detectors	talking about habits and routines	How often do you ...? frequency adverbs + prepositions of time	everyday activities
31 Talent scouts	asking about abilities	Can he/she ...?	abilities and skills
32 Room service	making requests	Can I have a/some ...?	hotel services
33 The restaurant game	asking for things	I'd like ..., please. Certainly, sir/madam. Sorry, sir/madam, it's off.	food
34 Blind date	inviting, accepting and refusing	Would you like to ...? I'd love to. I'm sorry I can't/I'm not free.	social life and entertainment
35 Noises off	asking about what's happening	Are you -ing ...? Yes, I am/No, I'm not.	everyday actions
36 Homelife	asking what's happening	Is she/he -ing ...? Yes, she/he is/No, she/he isn't. Are they -ing ...? Yes, they are/No, they aren't.	everyday actions
37 In the park	describing what's happening	What's he/she doing? He's/She's -ing ... . What are they doing? They're -ing	outdoor activities
38 Eyewitnesses	asking about and describing past events	was, were	houses
39 Last night	asking about past events	Did you ...? Yes, I did/No, I didn't.	entertainment and leisure
40 Souvenir shopping	talking about past events	I saw/went/ate/drank	holidays

Introduction

1 About games

A game is an activity with rules, a goal and an element of fun.

There are two kinds of games: *competitive games*, in which players or teams race to be the first to reach the goal, and *cooperative games*, in which players or teams work together towards a common goal. Both kinds are featured in this book.

The activities in this book fall into two types: *linguistic games* and *communicative games*. In linguistic games, the goal of the game is linguistic accuracy, i.e. producing a correct structure. Communicative games, however, are activities with a goal or aim that is not linguistic. Successful completion of the game will involve the carrying out of a task such as drawing in a route on a map, filling in a chart, or finding two matching pictures, rather than the correct production of a structure. However, in order to carry out this task it will be necessary to use language, and by careful construction of the task it will be possible to specify in advance what language will be required.

The emphasis in linguistic games is on accuracy, in communicative games the emphasis falls on fluency, on successful communication rather than on correctness of language. The games in this book thus cover the whole range of the accuracy-fluency spectrum. This raises the question of how and where they should be used in class. Games should be regarded as an integral part of the language syllabus, not as an amusing activity for Friday afternoon or for the end of term. They can provide as much concentrated controlled practice as a traditional drill or an opportunity for real communication at the freer end of the spectrum and thus constitute a bridge between the classroom and the real world

These games can be used at all stages of the progression from controlled to free practice, serving at one end of the range as a memory aid and repetition drill, at the other, as a chance to use language freely and as a means to an end rather than an end in itself. They can also serve as a diagnostic tool for the teacher, who can note areas of difficulty and take appropriate remedial action.

2 About this book

This book is a resource book of practice activities. The games have been designed to *practise*, not to introduce new language. The book assumes that introduction and explanation of the new language items have been done in the textbook or other course material that the teacher and class is following.

The games have been arranged following a structural/functional syllabus in the order in which they appear in most textbooks and courses at this level. The topic area, function, essential vocabulary and structures that the students will need are all listed at the beginning of each game. The teacher can thus use this book as supplementary practice material, selecting and discarding games as she chooses.

The games make use of a variety of techniques. Variety is important in language teaching, and a succession of games based on the same principles, though exciting and novel at first, would soon become boring. Techniques used include information gap, guessing, search, matching, exchanging, collecting, combining, arranging, and card games, board games, puzzles and role-play.

The simplest activities are based on the *information gap* principle. In these activities Student A has access to some information which is not held by Student B. Student B must acquire this information to complete a task successfully. This type of game may be *one-sided*, as in the above example, or *reciprocal*, where both players have information which they must pool to solve a common problem. The games may be played in pairs or small groups, where all the members of the group have some information.

Guessing games are a familiar variant on this principle. The player with the information deliberately withholds it, while others guess what it might be.

Search games are another variant, involving the whole class. In these games everyone in the class has one piece of information. Players must obtain all or a large amount of the information available to fill in a questionnaire or to solve a problem. Each student is thus simultaneously a giver and a collector of information.

Matching games are based on a different principle, but also involve a transfer of information. These games involve matching corresponding pairs of cards or pictures, and may be played as a whole class activity, where everyone must circulate until they find a partner with a corresponding card or picture; or as a pairwork or small group activity, where players must choose pictures or cards from a selection to match those chosen by their partner from the same selection; or as a card game on the 'snap' principle.

Matching-up games are based on a jigsaw or 'fitting together' principle. Each player in a group has a list of opinions, preferences, wants or possibilities. Through discussion and compromise the group must reach an agreement.

Exchanging games are based on the 'barter' principle. Players have certain articles, cards or ideas which they wish to exchange for others. The aim of the game is to make an exchange which is satisfactory to both sides.

In *collecting games*, players need to collect cards in order to complete a set. These may be played as a whole class activity, where players circulate freely, exchanging articles or cards at random, or as an ordinary card game.

Combining activities are those in which the players must act on certain information in order to arrange themselves in groups such as families or people spending holidays together.

Arranging games are also sometimes called *sequencing* or *ordering games*. These are games where the players must acquire information and act on it in order to arrange items in a specific order. Items to be arranged can be picture cards, events in a narrative, or even the players themselves!

3 Some practical considerations

A] Classroom management

There are three main types of activities in this book: *pairwork*, involving two partners, *small group work*, involving groups of three or four, and *whole class activities*, where everyone moves freely around the room. All these activities require some flexibility in the constitution of groups and organisation of the classroom.

For group work, divide the class into a combination of groups of three and groups of four. Any number will divide into a combination of threes and fours, for example, thirteen students will make three groups of three and one group of four, twenty-three students will make five groups of four and one group of three.

It is best to have the desks in a U-shape if possible. Students can then work with the person sitting next to them for pair work, and groups of threes and fours can easily be constituted by alternate pairs moving their chairs to the inner side of the U, opposite another pair. Whole class activities, which involve all the students circulating freely, can take place in the empty area in the centre of the U-shape. Simulation activities may involve special arrangements of furniture and suggestions are made in the Teacher's notes for these activities. If it is not possible to arrange desks in this way, this need not deter you! The traditional arrangement of front-facing desks can be easily adapted to pairwork, with people at adjoining desks working together, while small groups can be formed by two people turning their chairs round to face the people behind them. Whole class activities present a little more of a problem, but often there is a space big enough for the students to move around in at the front of the class, or desks can be pushed back to clear a space in the centre.

In most cases, whole class games have been designed so that half the class remains seated and only half is moving around so that teachers who experience a great deal of difficulty with the kind of games that require lots of students to move around, can play these games in a controlled way.

Games are best set up by demonstration rather than by lengthy explanation. The teacher should explain briefly what the game involves, hand out the photocopied cards, giving the students a little time to study them, and then demonstrate the game with one of the students in front of the class. It will be found that the idea of the game is probably easier for students to grasp from seeing the cards than from a verbal explanation, and that as they become more familiar with the idea of the games and the techniques used, any initial problems caused by unfamiliarity will quickly disappear. Where card games are played in small groups, teachers may like to hand out the appropriate pictorial Rules sheets to each group of students together with the card(s). You can then either let students 'read' the rules themselves while you circulate to deal with problems or, with less confident groups, take the whole class through each step of the rules. There is a reference in the Teacher's notes for each game to indicate where Rules sheets are provided. These are to be found at the back of the book, after the games material section, on pages 105-11.

The teacher's role in these activities is that of monitor and resource centre, moving from group to group, listening, supplying any necessary language, noting errors, but not interrupting or correcting as this impedes fluency and spoils the atmosphere. It is a good idea to carry paper and pen and to note any persistent errors or areas of difficulty. These can then be dealt with in a feedback session after the game. In many cases the game could then be played again with different partners or with different role cards.

The average length of time for the games in the book is about 15-20 minutes.

B] Resource management

The resources required for each game fall into two categories: reusable and disposable. Where a very small number of photocopies are needed for a whole class game or where students may write on their cards, it is best to treat these photocopies as disposable. There is no point, therefore, in collecting up the photocopies in order to use them with another class when the game is finished.

In contrast, some of the games in this book require a larger number of copies and an investment of the teacher's time in accurate copying, cutting up etc., so it is worthwhile thinking of these materials as reusable resources. For example, the pairwork and small group games require a set of cards for each pair or group of students in the class. The students will not need to write anything on the cards, and as these are mostly quiet games with only two to four people involved, the cards should reach the end of the game in much the same state as they began. It is worth, therefore, investing some time in making the photocopies into a permanent class set of materials. If you have the time and resources, obviously copying or pasting the materials onto card or laminating them would help preserve their shelf-life. If you don't have the time or the resources, however, this isn't absolutely necessary: I have sets of games materials copied only onto paper, that have done their duty in workshops all over the world and aren't much the worse for wear after five years. What is more important is providing a system to prevent the materials getting lost and disorganised. If you have a class set of ten sets of cards, for example, it is worth putting each set into an envelope clearly labelled with the name of the game and the number of cards. It is then the students' responsibility to collect up all the cards at the end of the game, check that they are all there, put them back into the envelope and hand them back to you. If two sets of cards are required for a game, keep them in two smaller envelopes inside the big one, and get the students to sort them back into their respective envelopes at the end of the game.

Finally, if you have no access to copying facilities at all, it is possible, though time-consuming, to make home-made versions of the materials by getting the students to work with you to draw and write the cards. You would need to give every student a sheet of paper and instruct them how to divide it up into squares. Then either dictate to the students what to draw or write in each square, or make large drawings of the cards on the board for them to copy. Ask the students to cut up the cards when they have finished and put them into an envelope. In this way you will have a reusable class set of materials. This is obviously time-consuming for you and the students, but initial effort will result in a set of materials that can be kept and reused, and students may be happy to cooperate if they know the result will lead to an enjoyable game.

4 The role of games in the language programme

The inclusion of games as an integral part of any language syllabus provides an opportunity for intensive language practice, offers a context in which language is used meaningfully and as a means to an end, and acts as a diagnostic tool for the teacher, highlighting areas of difficulty. Last, but certainly not least, although the above discussion has tended to focus on methodological considerations, one of the most important reasons for using games is simply that they are immensely enjoyable for both teacher and student.

Teacher's notes

1 Doppelganger

Type of activity
whole class; matching

Function practised
greetings and introductions

Structures
Hello.
My name is … .
What's your name?

Topic area
names

Essential vocabulary
no extra vocabulary needed

Materials and preparation

Copy the NAME CARDS. Cut up as many as you need for your class, making sure each name appears twice.

How to use the game

• Give out the name cards.

• Tell the students that somewhere in the class is someone with the same name.

• **The object of the game is to find someone with the same name.**

• To do this they will have to stand up and move around the class, introducing themselves and asking for names until they find someone with the same name.

• When they have found that person they can sit down.

Demonstration

Demonstrate how to do this by taking a matching pair of name cards. Give one to a student and keep one yourself. Ask two or three other students for their names and make a pantomime of looking at your own card and shaking your head. Then 'find' the student with the same name and make a pantomime of looking delighted. Show the class the names are the same.

Classroom language

Here's a card.
This is a name.
It's your name.

This is your name. *(give a card to a student)*
And this is my name. *(show the class your card)*
I must find the same name.
Hello. My name's … . What's your name?
No. It's not the same. *(shake your head and look disappointed; show the two cards to the class)*
Ah look! It's the same! *(look excited and show the two cards to the class)*
Now we can sit down! *(demonstrate)*
OK, everybody, stand up.
Find the same name.
When you find the same name, sit down.

Variation

If you have a new class and they don't yet know each others' (real) names, play this variation.

• Ask everyone to write their names on a piece of paper.

• Collect these up.

• Redistribute the names, making sure no one gets their own name.

• **The object of the game is to find the person whose name is on the piece of paper.**

• To do this, they will have to stand up and go round the class, telling everyone their (real) name and asking for names:
'Hello, my name's … . What's your name?'

• When they find the person whose name is on their paper, they should give them the paper.

• When they have given away their paper and got their own name back, they should sit down.

2 Spelling lotto

Type of activity
small group; matching

Function practised
spelling words

Structures
none

Topic area
letters of the alphabet

Essential vocabulary
names of the letters

(The following words are used in the game, chosen to include all the letters in the alphabet, but also because they are either simple, basic, useful vocabulary, or words that may be the same in a number of languages: *table, chair, house, book, pen, girl, boy, man, dog, fish, zoo, jam, television, queen, X-ray, window.* Learning the words is not the point of the game, but it may be a useful by-product.)

Materials and preparation

Mentally divide the students in your class into groups of three or four.
Copy one set of WORD CARDS and one set of LOTTO BOARDS for each group.
There is a pictorial Rules sheet for this game on page 106. Make copies for each group after making the changes for this game that are noted there.

NOTE   If you want to make the game harder or want your students to learn the vocabulary, make one copy of the boards, tippex out the words underneath the pictures, and then use this as your copymaster.

How to use the game

- Divide your class into groups of three or four.

- Give out a set of lotto boards and a set of word cards to each group. (For groups of three, remove one lotto board and the corresponding word cards.)

- They should take a board each and place the word cards face down in the middle.

- **The object of the game is for students to cover all the pictures on their lotto boards with matching word cards.**

- The first player takes a word card and spells it out to the group.

- The player with the matching picture on her board should ask for the card and cover her picture with the word card.

- Then it is the next player's turn to take and spell a word card.

- The player who covers all his pictures first is the winner.

Demonstration
Demonstrate how to do this with the whole class.
Ask them to look at their lotto boards.
Take a word card yourself and spell it out.
Ask those who have the same word to raise their hands.
Then get the class to play a demonstration round (or two) of the game under your supervision, before letting them play in groups by themselves.

Classroom language

Here are some boards.
Take one board each.
Here are some cards.
Put the cards face down on the table. *(demonstrate)*
Look at your boards.
Listen. I'm going to **spell** a word.
What is the word?
Who's got the picture? Put up your hands.
OK. Good.
Now. Listen to your numbers. *(number the players in each group 1, 2, 3, 4)*
Number 1, pick up a card. *(demonstrate)*
Have you got a card? OK. Good.
Now, spell the word.
Who's got the picture?
Give the card to that person. *(demonstrate)*
Now Number 2, pick up a card. *(etc.)*

3 Ladybird bingo

Type of activity
small group; matching

Function practised
numbers

Structures
none

Topic area
numbers

Essential vocabulary
numbers 1-20

Materials and preparation

Mentally divide your class into groups of three or four.
Copy one set of LOTTO BOARDS and one set of CARDS per group.
There is a pictorial Rules sheet for this game on page 106. Make copies for each group after making the changes that are noted there.

How to use the game

- Divide your class into groups of three or four.

- Give one set of lotto boards and one set of cards to each group.

- They should take a board each and place the cards face down in the middle.

- **The object of the game is for students to cover all the pictures on their boards with matching cards.**

- The first player takes a card, counts the spots on the ladybird and tells the group the number.

- The player with the matching picture should ask for the card and cover her picture with the card. (The player who asks first gets the card.) In groups of three, if no one has the matching pictures, discard the card.

- Then it is the next player's turn to take a card and count the number of spots.

- The player who covers the most pictures at the end of the game is the winner.

Demonstration

Demonstrate how to do this with the whole class.
Ask them to look at their boards.
Take a card yourself. Show it to the class and count the spots.
Ask those who have the same picture on their board to raise their hands.
Then get the class to play a demonstration round (or two) of the game under your supervision, before letting them play in groups by themselves.

Classroom language

Here are some boards.
Take one board each.
Here are some cards.
Put the cards face down on the table. *(demonstrate)*
Look. I'm going to take a card. Look at the ladybird. I'm going to **count** the spots *(count, pointing to the spots)*
Now look at your boards.
Who has the same picture? Put up your hands. Say 'ME!'
OK. Good.
Now. Listen to your numbers. *(number the players in each group 1, 2, 3, 4)*
Number 1, pick up a card *(demonstrate)*
Have you got a card?
OK. Good.
Now, count the spots. Say the number. *(one etc.)*
Who has the same picture? Shout 'ME!'
Who is first? *(find out who was the first person in each group)*
Give the card to that person. *(demonstrate)*
Now Number 2, pick up a card. *(etc.)*

4 Clockmatch

Type of activity
small group; matching

Function practised
asking and telling the time

Structures
What's the time?
It's (twelve o'clock).

Topic area
time

Essential vocabulary
numbers to 25; *o'clock, half past, a quarter to, a quarter past*

Materials and preparation

Mentally divide your class into groups of three or four.
Copy and cut up two (or three for the more competitive version) sets of CLOCK CARDS for each group.
There is a pictorial Rules sheet for this game on page 109. Make copies for each group after making the changes that are noted there.

How to use the game

- Divide your class into groups of three or four and seat each group round a table.

- Give each group one set of clock cards.

- They should deal out the cards equally among them (3-4 cards each).

- They should look at their cards.

- Then give each group the second set of cards. These are to be placed face down in the middle.

- The first player begins by picking up a card from the pile on the table and looking at it.

- The others ask, 'What's the time?'

- The first player must tell them.

- The player with the matching card can throw away both cards.

- Then it is his turn to pick up the next card from the pile.

- **The object of the game is to get rid of all your cards.**

- The player who gets rid of his cards first is the winner.

Demonstration

Demonstrate how to play the game by doing the first round with the whole class.
Get them to deal out their cards.
Check they've done this, then get them to pick them up and look at them.

Then give them the second pile to put in the middle.
Name a player in each group to begin.
Tell them to take a card from the pile and look at it, but not to show the others.
Get the others to ask, 'What's the time?'
Get Player 1 to reply.
Then ask, 'Who has the same card?'
Ask them to put up their hands.
Then get the player with the matching card in each group to take both cards and discard them.
That player is then the next one to pick up a card from the pile.

NOTE If you want a more competitive version of the game, copy three sets of cards instead of two for each group and shuffle two sets together in the pack to be dealt out. For every card that is picked up, there will be two matching cards, and the 'trick' will go to the player who calls out the time first.

Classroom language

Here are some cards.
Deal out the cards. *(demonstrate)*
Good. Pick up the cards. You can look at them. *(demonstrate)*
Here are some more cards.
Put them in the middle. *(giving a pile to each group)*
X, Y, Z. *(naming a student in each group)* You begin.
Pick up a card from the pile. *(demonstrate)*
Look at it but **don't show it to the others**! *(demonstrate)*
OK. Everybody ask, 'What's the time?'
X, Y, Z, tell the time, 'It's ... .'
Who has the same card? Put up your hands.
Good. You can take both cards. *(demonstrate)*
Throw them away, like this. *(demonstrate)*
OK. Good. Now you can pick up a card.

5 Lost in the post

Type of activity
whole class; matching

Function practised
asking for and giving personal information

Structures
What's your name?
What's your address?

Topic area
names and addresses

Essential vocabulary
Mr, Mrs, Miss, Ms, road, street; numbers
plus for recognition only: *postman, house, letter, address*

Materials and preparation
Mentally divide your class in half.
Copy and cut up that number of LETTER CARDS and their matching NAME CARDS.

How to use the game

• Pre-teach *postman, house, letter* and *address* with a simple picture on the board.

• Divide your class into two groups.

• Ask one group to come to the front.

• The other group should stay in their seats.

• Give the seated group a name card each.

• Tell them, 'This is your house. This is your name and this is your address.'

• Give the standing group a letter each. Tell them, 'You are postmen. Here is a letter. Find the right house.'

• **The object of the game is for all the postmen to deliver their letters to the right houses.**

• When they have finished, you can play again, changing roles, so that postmen become householders.

Demonstration
Take a 'letter' from one of the 'postmen' and demonstrate going to a 'house'.
Ask, 'What's your name? What's your address?'
Shake your head to show it's the wrong house and try another 'house'.

Classroom language

Look. This is a postman. *(drawing a picture on the board)*
He's got a letter. On the letter is a name and an address. The postman is taking the letter to this house. *(label postman, letter, name, address, and house)*
Listen to your number. *(give all students a number 1 or 2)*
Who is number 1? Put up your hands.
OK. All the 1s come to the front. *(gesture)*
All the 2s stay sitting. *(gesture)*
This is your house. This is your name and this is your address. *(giving out the name cards)*
You are a postman. Here is a letter.
Find the house. Like this. *(demonstrate)*
What's your name? And what's your address?
Oh! It's not the right house. *(look disappointed and show the 'letter')*
You try now. Find the right house.

6 Wedding photos

Type of activity
pairwork; information gap

Function practised
asking and saying who someone is

Structures
Who's this/that?
This is/That's (Mary/John). She's/He's my (sister/brother).

Topic area
family members

Essential vocabulary
mother, father, sister, brother, aunt, uncle, cousin, grandmother, grandfather

Materials and preparation

Mentally divide your class in half.
Copy and cut up enough WEDDING PHOTOS for all the class plus one for you.
Copy and cut up enough FAMILY TREE A CARDS for one half of the class plus one for you and enough FAMILY TREE B CARDS for the other half.

How to use the game

• Divide the students into pairs A and B.

• Give everyone a wedding photo card.

• Tell them that this is a wedding picture: A's sister is marrying B's brother.

• A's family is on one side of the picture and B's family is on the other side.

• Give all the As the family tree A card and all the Bs the family tree B card.

• Tell them this is their family.

• **The object of the game is to find out who all the people in the photo are and to write their names in on the photo.**

• To do this, they will have to ask each other, 'Who's that?' and answer, e.g. 'That's Jane. She's my mother.'

Demonstration

Demonstrate how to do this by taking your wedding photo and the family tree A card, calling up one B student to the front and playing a demonstration game. Put both photos on the table so you can both see them. Point to one figure in the photo and ask the student, 'Who's that?'
Give her time to look at her family tree and work it out. Prompt her with the reply if necessary - 'That's ... . She's/He's my ... .'
Then show the class how to write in the name on the photo.

Then prompt B to ask you a question, 'Who's that?' and get her to write in the name on the photo.

Classroom language

Listen. A. *(point to one student)* B. *(point to the student next to her)* You two work together.
A, B. You two work together. *(continue right round the class until all the class is divided up into pairs)*
Look. Here is a wedding photo. *(give out the photos)*
Who is A? *(get them to raise their hands)* This is your sister. *(point)*
Who is B? *(get them to raise their hands)* This is your brother. *(point)*
A's sister is marrying B's brother.
This is your family. *(giving out the family trees A to the As)*
Don't show it to B. *(mime keeping it secret)*
This is your family. *(giving out the family trees B to the Bs)*
Don't show it to A. *(mime keeping it secret)*
Who are the people in the photo? Ask each other. Like this.
Come up to the front, please.
Put your photo on the table. Good.
Who's that? *(pointing to a person in the photo)*
Look at your family tree. Don't show me. *(when she answers, write in the name repeating the answer)*
Good. Now you ask me, 'Who's that?' *(give the answer and get her to write it in)*
OK? Now you do it. Work together.

7 Mine!

Type of activity
small group; collecting

Function practised
asking and saying who things belong to

Structures
Whose is this/are these?
Mine! My (brother's).
Possessive *'s: brother's, sister's, mother's, father's*

Topic area
family, clothes

Essential vocabulary
family: *mother, father, sister, brother*
plus for recognition only: *sock, shoe, glove, earring, jacket*

Materials and preparation

Mentally divide your class into groups of three or four.
Copy and cut up one set of FAMILY CARDS and one set

of CLOTHES CARDS for each group.
There is a pictorial Rules sheet for this game on page 107. Make copies for each group.

How to use the game

- Divide the class into groups of three or four.

- Give each group a set of family cards and a set of clothes cards.

- Each student should take one family card.

- They should put the clothes cards face down in a pile in the middle.

- Player 1 takes a clothes card and holds it up saying, 'Whose is this?/Whose are these?'

- The players should look at their family cards. Every family member has a piece of clothing missing. If the clothes card corresponds to any of the items of clothing missing from their pictures, they can claim it saying, 'Mine!/My mother's/father's/sister's/brother's.'

- **The object of the game is to complete the family card with the five missing items of clothing.**

- The player who does so first is the winner.

Demonstration
Demonstrate how to play the game by playing the first round with the whole class.
Get the students to look at their family cards first and say what's missing: 'My glove, my brother's shoe(s)' etc.
Take a clothes card and hold it up so everyone can see, saying, 'Whose is this?'
Get the students to look at their family cards to see whose it is.
Prompt students to give the answer, 'Mine!/My mother's/father's/sister's/brother's.'
Demonstrate that they can take the card and put it on their family card.
Repeat with another card if necessary.
Then get them to carry on in their groups.

Classroom language

Here are some family cards.
Look at my family card.
Some clothes are missing. Look! My glove is missing. My brother's shoe is missing.
Look at your family card.
What's missing?
Here's a clothes card. What is it? *(holding up a shoe)*
Good. It's a (shoe).
Whose (shoe) is it?
Yours? OK. Take the (shoe) and put it on your card.
Good. Now you play.
Take the clothes cards and put them in the middle, like this.
Take the top card.
Show it to the others, like this. *(demonstrate)*

Say, 'Whose is this?' or 'Whose are these?'
Answer, 'Mine!' or 'My mother's' or 'My sister's'.
Then take the card and put it on your family card.
OK. Off you go.

8 National dress

Type of activity
whole class (or small group); matching

Function practised
asking about country and nationality

Structures
What's your name?
My name is (Nisha).
Where are you from?
I'm from (India). I'm (Indian).
Is this yours?

Topic area
country and nationality

Essential vocabulary
India/Indian, Mexico/Mexican, The Netherlands/Dutch, England/English, France/French, Germany/German, China/ Chinese, The USA/American, Japan/Japanese, Switzerland/Swiss, Spain/Spanish, Saudi Arabia/Saudi Arabian
(It is not necessary to know the the names of the clothes in order to play the game.)

Materials and preparation

Mentally divide your class in half.
Copy and cut up enough COUNTRY CARDS for half the class and enough matching DRESS CARDS for the other half.

How to use the game

- Divide the class in half.

- Ask half the class to come to the front.

- Give this half the dress cards.

- The others can remain seated.

- Give them the country cards.

- Tell the students who are standing that they have an object that belongs to someone in the class.

- **The object of the game is to find who the object belongs to and give it back.**

- To do this, the students who have the dress cards should move around the class, asking the other students, 'What's your name? Where are you from?' until they find someone they think is the owner of the object. Then they can ask, 'Is this yours?'

- When they have found the owner, they should give the card to them and then sit down.

- When you have played the game once, you can play it again so that the students who were sitting are now moving around looking for people.

Demonstration

Demonstrate how to play, by taking one of the dress cards and going up to one of the seated students and asking, 'What's your name? Where are you from?' Show them your card and ask, 'Is this yours?' Look disappointed when they say, 'No', and move on to repeat with another student.

NOTE   If you want to play this game in a more static version in small groups rather than as a whole class, it can be played as a card game. Follow the instructions for *Game 14 Tools for the job* (substituting country cards for job cards and dress cards for equipment cards).

Classroom language

Can you stand up, please.
Come to the front of the class, please.
Here is a card.
This is your name.
This is your country.
Here is a card for you.
This belongs to someone here.
Find the person.
Like this: *(demonstrate)*
Hello. What's your name?
And where are you from?
Is this yours? No? *(shake your head; look disappointed; move on)*

9 Don't worry!

Type of activity
pairwork; matching

Function practised
asking about feelings

Structures
Are you (hungry)?
Yes, I am/No, I'm not.
Here you are.

Topic area
feelings

Essential vocabulary
hungry, thirsty, cold, hot, tired, sad, happy, bored, ill, worried, uncomfortable, angry

Materials and preparation

Mentally divide your class into pairs.
Copy and cut up one set of FEELINGS CARDS and one set of OBJECT CARDS for each pair.

How to use the game

- Divide the students into pairs, A and B.

- Give each pair a set of object cards.

- They should spread these out on the table and look at them.

- Then give each pair a set of feelings cards.

- They should place these face down in a pile in the middle.

- Student A picks up a card from the feelings pile.

- Student B must try to guess the feeling by asking, 'Are you ...?'

- When she has guessed correctly, she should take the appropriate object card and match it with student A's card (e.g. *drink* for thirsty, *pills* for ill etc.).

- **The object of the game is to match all the cards correctly.**

Demonstration

Demonstrate how to play by playing with the whole class. Divide students into pairs and give each pair the pack of object cards only.
Get them to spread these out on the desk and look at them.
Tell them, 'I'm hungry.' Ask them what they would give you. Try again with *thirsty, worried, uncomfortable.* Go on till they seem confident.
Then take a card from the feelings pile. Hold it so they can't see it but you can.
Get them to guess what you are feeling. Prompt them by asking, 'Are you ...?'
When they have guessed, get them to hold up the object they would give you.

Classroom language

Here are some cards.
Spread them out. *(demonstrate)* Look at them.
I feel hungry. Help me! Have you got something for me?
Thank you!
Now I feel thirsty. *(etc.)*
Thank you!
Right. Now I've got a card.
You can't see the picture. You must guess. *(prompt them: 'Are you hungry? Are you thirsty?', etc.)*
No, I'm not. *(etc.)*
Yes! I am! Help me! Have you got something for me?

Oh. Thank you! *(take the card and put it with your picture to show they match; put both cards down together)*
Now you play together.
Here are some cards.
A, B, C. *(indicate students)* Begin.
Take a card. **Don't show it to the others!**
X, Y, Z. *(indicate students)* Guess.

10 Identity parade

Type of activity
pairwork; matching

Function practised
describing people

Structures
Is he/she (tall)?
Yes, she/he is. No, she/he isn't.

Topic area
people's appearances

Essential vocabulary
tall, thin, fat, small, old, young, strong, beautiful, handsome, ugly

Materials and preparation
Make two copies of the pictures for each pair of students in the class.
Cut these up into separate cards.

How to use the game
- Divide the students into pairs, A and B.

- Give the As a set of pictures.

- They should spread these out in front of them.

- Give the Bs a set of separate picture cards.

- They should put these face down on the table and take three.

- They must not show them to the As.

- **The object of the game is for the As to find which three criminals B has seen.**

- To do this, they will have to ask questions, e.g. 'Is he tall? Is he thin?' etc., until they can match the pictures.

Demonstration
Demonstrate by playing the game with the whole class.
Divide the students into pairs, but only give them one set of cards.
Ask them to lay these out on the table.

Take three cards yourself. Tell the students you saw three men robbing a house. The students are police officers. You are going to describe the men to them. Describe the first picture, e.g.: 'He's tall. He's strong etc.' Ask them to show you which picture it is. If they choose the wrong one, give them more information.
Get them to take the picture and put it to one side on the desk.
Then get them to ask you questions about the next picture: 'Is he tall? Is he thin?' etc.
When they guess, get them to take their picture and place it next to the first picture.
Repeat with the third picture if necessary, then give out the second set of cards to the Bs and ask them to take three. Get them to continue in pairs.

Classroom language
Here are some pictures.
Spread them out on the desk. *(demonstrate)*
Look at them.
Last night, I saw three men robbing a house. *(take three pictures)*
You are police officers.
Listen. I'm going to tell you about the first man: 'He's tall. He's strong. He's young.'
Which picture is it?
No. That man is ugly. This man is handsome.
Which picture?
Good.
Take the picture.
Put it over here. *(demonstrate)*
Now the next picture. This time you ask questions *(prompt)*: 'Is he ...?'
Good.
Take the picture.
Put it over here, next to the first picture, like this.
Now you go on.
Here are the pictures for you. Choose three but **don't show them to your friend!**
Now you go on. Ask questions and find the three men.

11 Class colours

Type of activity
whole class; search game

Function practised
asking about preferences

Structures
What colour is/are (your favourite drink/clothes)?

Topic area
colours

Essential vocabulary
red, blue, green, yellow, brown, black, white, orange, purple, pink, grey
plus for recognition only: *favourite, drink, fruit, ice cream, sweet, football team, flower, clothes, animal*
or: *flag, postbox, police car, uniform, passport, banknote, taxi, bus*

Materials and preparation

Choose which questionnaire to do. (B will only work if you have a multinational class!)
Make one copy of the QUESTIONNAIRE for every student in the class.

How to use the game

- Give out a copy of the questionnaire to every student (make sure they know the recognition vocabulary as well as the colours).

- Ask them to take a pen and the questionnaire and to complete the questionnaire by asking people the questions.

- **The object of the game is to complete the questionnaire. The rules are: 1. Get eight different people's names. 2. Get eight different colours.**

- To do this, they will have to move around the room, asking the questions until they have a different person's name and a different colour in each gap.

Demonstration
Demonstrate how to do this by writing up a questionnaire on the board.
Ask questions to different students, making it clear that a different name and a different colour must appear in each box.

Classroom language
Here is a questionnaire.
Ask the questions, like this. *(do the demonstration on the board)*
Take the paper and a pen.
Stand up.
Ask questions.

Write the answers on the paper, like this.
You must have eight different names here.
You must have eight different colours here.
When you finish, sit down.
OK, everyone?
Off you go!

NOTE If you have a multinational class, you might like to try questionnaire B. They should get answers from three different nationalities.

12 What is it?

Type of activity
small group; guessing

Function practised
describing objects/shapes

Structures
Is it (round)?
Yes, it is/No, it isn't.
Are they (round)?
Yes, they are/No, they aren't.

Topic area
size and shape

Essential vocabulary
round, square, big, small, thick, thin, long, short, tall

Materials and preparation

Mentally divide your class into groups of three or four.
Copy and cut up two sets of pictures for each group.
There is a pictorial Rules sheet for this game on page 110. Make copies for each group after making the changes that are noted there.

How to use the game

- Divide your class into groups of three or four and seat them round a table.

- Give each group two sets of pictures.

- They should spread out one set on the table, face up.

- They should put the others in a pile in the middle, face down.

- Player 1 takes a card from the pile and keeps it hidden from the other students.

- The others try to guess what it is by asking, 'Is it big/small/round/square (etc.)?'

- Tell the students they can't ask questions such as 'Is it a plate/picture/book?' etc.

- **The object of the game is to find the corresponding card from those spread out on the table.**

- The player who guesses first should pick up the matching card from the table and claim the two cards as a trick.

- At the end, the player with the most tricks is the winner.

Demonstration

Demonstrate by playing a round with the whole class.
Divide the class into groups and give out one set of cards only.
Ask them to spread them out on the table and look at them.
Take a card yourself and hold it so you can see it but the class cannot.
Get them to ask questions: 'Is it big/small/round/square?' etc.
When they think they know what it is, get them to pick up the matching card from the table and hold it up.

Classroom language

Here are some cards.
Spread them out on the table. *(demonstrate)*
Look at them.
I've got a card here. *(demonstrate)*
Guess what it is. Ask questions *(prompt them:* 'Is it big? Is it small? Is it round? You go on.'*)*
No, it isn't.
Yes, it is!
Do you know what it is?
Which picture is it?
Hold it up.
Good!
OK. Now you play.
Here are some cards. Put them in a pile.
X, Y, Z. *(name one student in each group)* You begin.
Pick up a card from the pile. *(demonstrate)*
Don't show it to the others! *(demonstrate)*
Now ask questions.

13 Happy Birthday

Type of activity
whole class; search game

Function practised
asking and saying when birthdays are

Structures
When is your birthday?
It's in (February).
It's on (February the 28th).

Topic area
numbers, months

Essential vocabulary
birthday; numbers to 31, months of the year; names of presents as required by the students (e.g. *book, chocolates, flowers* etc.)

Materials and preparation

Copy and cut up the PRESENTS CARDS. You will need one for every student.

How to use the game

- Give each student a 'present'.

- Ask them to write the date of their birthday on the label.

- Then collect up the presents and redistribute them at random so that each student has a different present.

- This time, ask them to imagine what is in the parcel (e.g. a book, a box of chocolates, a parrot in a cage) and to write on the back of the card what is in the parcel.

- Go round helping them with vocabulary.

- **The object of the game is for everyone to find out who their present is for and to give it to them.**

- To do this, they will have to stand up and move around the class asking, 'When is your birthday?' until they find the person who owns the present.

- They should then give them the present, explaining what it is.

Demonstration

Demonstrate how to play the search part of the game, by taking a present yourself and trying to find its owner.
Ask a couple of students, 'When is your birthday?'
Shake your head and look disappointed when the date is not the same as the one on the label.

Classroom language

This is a present. *(hold one up and show them)*
It's for you.
Write your birthday on the label, like this. *(show them with a sketch on the board)*
Now give them all to me. Sorry! *(collect all the cards)*
Here you are. Now you've got a new present. *(give out the cards)*
What is it? A book? Chocolates? Flowers? A cat? What do you think?
Write on the back, like this. *(demonstrate and then go round to help them)*
Finished? Good!
Look at the birthday on the label. *(show them)*
Who is the present for?
Find the student. Ask, 'When is your birthday?' like this. *(demonstrate by taking one student's present and asking a few people when their birthday is)*
When you find the student, give them the present.
Say 'Happy Birthday!' *(mime giving the present)*

14 Tools for the job

Type of activity
small group; matching

Function practised
asking about jobs

Structures
What do you do?/What's your job?
I'm a (doctor).
Is this yours?

Topic area
jobs

Essential vocabulary
doctor, cook, teacher, dancer, police officer, firefighter, builder, pilot, waitress, nurse, scientist, mechanic (students do not need to know the names of the equipment)

Materials and preparation

Mentally divide your class into groups of three or four.
Copy and cut up one set of JOB CARDS and one set of EQUIPMENT CARDS for each group.
There is a pictorial Rules sheet for this game on page 109. Make copies for each group after making the changes that are noted there.

How to use the game

- Divide the class into groups of three or four and seat them round a table.

- Give each group a set of equipment cards.

- Ask them to deal them out.

- Players can pick their cards up and look at them.

- Give each group a set of job cards.

- These should be placed face down in a pile in the middle.

- Player 1 should pick up a card from the pile.

- The others should ask her, 'What do you do?'

- She should reply with the name of the job, 'I'm a ... .'

- The player with the matching piece of equipment can then give it to her, saying, 'Is this yours?'

- Both cards can be discarded and the second player can then pick a card from the job pile.

- **The object of the game is to get rid of all the cards in your hand.**

- The player who does this first is the winner.

Demonstration
Demonstrate how to play the game by doing the first round with the whole class.
Give the equipment cards to each group.
Get them to deal out their cards.
Check they've done this, then get them to pick them up and look at them.
Then give each group the job cards to put in a pile in the middle.
Name a player in each group to begin.
Tell him to take a card from the pile and look at it, but not to show it to the others!
Get the others to ask, 'What do you do?'
Get Player 1 to reply, 'I'm a ... .'
Then ask, 'Who has something for him?'
Ask them to put up their hands.
Then get the player with the matching equipment card in each group to show their card.
If they are right, they can throw it away.
That player is then the next one to pick up a card from the job pile.

Classroom language

Here are some cards.
Deal out the cards. *(demonstrate)*
Good. Pick up the cards. You can look at them. *(demonstrate)*
Here are some more cards. Put them in the middle. *(giving a pile to each group)*
X, Y, Z. *(naming a student in each group)* You begin.
Pick up a card from the pile. *(demonstrate)*
Look at it **but don't show it to the others**! *(demonstrate)*
OK. Everybody ask, 'What do you do?'
X, Y, Z, tell them, 'I'm a ... .'
Look at your cards. Who has something for him?
Put up your hands.
Good. You can throw away your card. *(demonstrate)*
OK. Good. Now you can pick up a card.

15 School photo

Type of activity
pairwork; information gap

Function practised
asking about jobs

Structures
What does (X) do (now)?
He's/She's a (bus driver).

Topic area
jobs

Essential vocabulary
bus driver, doctor, teacher, journalist, businessman, dentist, cook, pilot, burglar, pop singer, filmstar, police officer

Materials and preparation

Mentally divide your class in half.
Copy SCHOOL PHOTO A for one half of the class and SCHOOL PHOTO B for the other half.

NOTE   Before you photocopy, write in a year on the two photos (19– –) that is about 15 years before the year in which you are actually doing the activity.

How to use the game

• Divide the students into pairs A and B.

• Give out school photo A to the As and school photo B to the Bs.

• Tell them this was their infant class in 19– – (i.e. the date you wrote in on your photocopy).

• **The object of the game is to find out what everyone's job is now.**

• To do this, they will have to ask each other questions, e.g. 'What does John do now?'

• When their partner answers, 'He's a doctor', they should write it in on the photo.

Demonstration
Demonstrate how to play by doing the first question with the whole class.
Ask them all to look at John. Ask the students who know what John does now to put up their hands. (The As will put up their hands.)
Ask them what he does and then show the Bs how to write it in on the photo by doing a quick sketch on the board.

16 Packing

Type of activity
pairwork; information gap

Function practised
asking and saying where things are

Structures
Where's/are the (map/tickets)?
It's/They're in/on/under/next to/near/in front of/behind the (sofa).

Topic area
holidays and travel

Essential vocabulary
tickets, passports, money, travellers' cheques, map, wallet, bag, guidebook, rucksack, suitcase, sofa, table, chair, floor

Materials and preparation

Mentally divide your class in half.
Copy and cut up enough ROOM A CARDS for one half of the class and enough ROOM B CARDS for the other half.

How to use the game

• Divide the class into pairs A and B.

• Give the As the room A cards and the Bs the room B cards.

• **The object of the game is for the As to find the things they need for going on holiday (pictured below their drawing) and the Bs to find the things they need (pictured below their drawing) and to draw them in on their pictures.**

• To do this, they will have to ask their partner, 'Where's/Where are the ...?', listen carefully to what their partner tells them and draw it in on their room.

Demonstration
Demonstrate how to do this, by taking a room A card, calling one B student up to the front and playing one round with her. Tell her you are both packing to go on holiday but you can't find the things you need. Ask her

where the passports are. When she tells you, mime drawing it in on your paper. Then tell the pairs to go on by themselves.

Classroom language

Work in pairs.
You two together, you two, you two. *(etc.)*
Here is a picture of a room. *(giving out the pictures)*
Look at it **but don't show it to your partner**!
You are going on holiday.
(talking to an A student) You need tickets, passport, money, travellers' cheques and a map. *(show them in the pictures below the room)*
But where are they?
Ask your partner where they are, like this. *(ask a B student to come up)*
Sonia, where are the passports? Do you know?
Thank you.
Now draw it in. *(show them)*
OK. Now play together.

17 Something old, something new

Type of activity
pairwork; information gap

Function practised
describing rooms

Structures
There is/isn't a (sofa).
There are some (cushions).
There aren't any (cushions).
prepositions: *near, next to, on*

Topic area
rooms and furniture

Essential vocabulary
sofa, cushions, curtains, rug, table, chair, television, bookcase, bed, desk, picture, cupboard, chest of drawers, boxes, lamp, bunk bed; new, different

Materials and preparation

Mentally divide your class in half.
Make enough copies of the OLD LIVING ROOM CARD and the OLD BEDROOM CARD for the whole class.
Make enough copies of the NEW LIVING ROOM CARD and the NEW BEDROOM CARD for half the class.

How to use the game

• Divide your class into pairs A and B.

• Give the As the pictures of the old living room.

• Give the Bs the pictures of the old bedroom.

• Tell them this is their old living room/bedroom.

• Then give the As the new living room card and the Bs the new bedroom card.

• Tell them that things are now different. Now it looks like this.

• How many differences can they see?

• Give the students a little time to work on their own studying their pictures. (There are about eight differences in each set of pictures.)

• Then give the As the old bedroom and the Bs the old living room.

• Tell them this is their partner's old room. They haven't seen the new one. Ask their partner about the differences: 'What's new? What's different?'

• **The object of the game is to find all the changes their partner has made in their new room.**

Demonstration
Demonstrate how to play the pairwork activity by doing the first round with one A student.
Tell them something about the new bedroom, e.g. 'There's a new desk near the door.' Get them to put a cross on the picture where the change is.
Then ask the student, 'What's different?' Prompt or remodel his answer if necessary. Put a cross on your picture where the change is.

Classroom language

This is your old living room. *(giving out pictures)*
This is your old bedroom. *(giving out pictures)*
Now it's different.
Now it looks like this. *(giving out pictures)*
Don't show it to your partner!
What's different? How many differences can you see?
This is your partner's old room.
You don't know the new room.
Ask your partner, 'What's different?'
Ask and answer like this: *(choose one A student)* 'In my bedroom, there's a new desk near the door.'
Put a cross on the picture.
Now I'll ask you, 'What's different in your living room?' *(help the student with the answer if necessary and put a cross in on your picture)*
OK. Now you play together.

18 My home town

Type of activity

whole class; search

Function practised

asking about town features

Structures

Is there a (library)? Yes, there is/No, there isn't.
Are there any (cafés)? Yes, there are/No, there aren't.

Topic area

town features

Essential vocabulary

library, bookshop, clothes shop, pub, café, restaurant, swimming pool, sports centre, park, theatre, cinema, disco

Materials and preparation

Make one copy of each of the four TOWN PLANS.
Make enough copies of the QUESTIONNAIRE for about two thirds of your class.

How to use the game

- Divide your class into roughly one third (group A) and two thirds (group B). (There should be at least four students in Group A. If you have more than four, group the students in Group A into pairs. If you have more than eight, divide the whole class in half and play the game in two separate groups.)

- Divide group A into four (subgroups). Give each a town plan.

- Give each student in Group B a questionnaire.

- Give the As a little time to study their plans and invent a name for their town and the Bs a little time to fill in their questionnaires.

- Then ask group B to stand up while group A remain seated (if they are seated close together, move them out into four separate areas of the classroom).

- Explain to group B that the students sitting down are in four different towns.

- Ask group A for the names of their towns.

- Tell them that group B are looking for a town to live in.

- **The object of the game is for the people in group B to find the town they like best.**

- To do this, they will have to move around the room asking the 'townspeople' in group A, 'Is there a ... in your town? Are there any ...s in your town?' until they find the one they like best.

- When they have found a 'town', they should stay there.

- When everyone has found a town, do a count of the inhabitants.

- Which town is the most popular?

Demonstration

Demonstrate how to play, by writing up your questionnaire with ticked priorities on the board for everyone to see.

Then demonstrate going to each of the four towns asking, e.g. 'Are there any bookshops?' (or whatever your highest priority is).

If the answer is no, shake your head sadly and tell the students, 'I don't want to live there.'

Go on till you find a town with bookshops, then ask about another priority.

Continue until you find a town you feel happy with and tell the class, 'I'm happy here. I want to live here.'

Classroom language

You are group A.
You live in this town. Give it a name.
Here is a map of your town.
You are group B.
Here is a questionnaire for you.
What is important for you? Tick five things.
(demonstrate)
OK. Now group B, stand up.
You want to live in a new town.
Here are four towns. *(point them out)*
Which is best for you?
Look for a town, like this.
Look, this is my questionnaire. *(put it on the board)*
I want a town with bookshops, a cinema, a theatre, pubs and a swimming pool.
Ask questions, like this. *(demonstrate playing the game until you find your town)*
OK, everyone?
Now you ask questions. Find your favourite town.
When you find a good town, stay there.

19 Mother Hubbard

Type of activity
pairwork; information gap

Function practised
asking about existence and quantity

Structures
Is there any (flour)?
How much (sugar) is there?
How many (eggs) are there?

Topic area
food and weights

Essential vocabulary
flour, sugar, eggs, butter, apples, milk, cheese, tomato, litre, grams, 100, 250, 500, a little

Materials and preparation

Mentally divide your class in half.
Make that number of copies of the CUPBOARD 1 CARDS and CUPBOARD 2 CARDS and the RECIPE 1 CARDS and RECIPE 2 CARDS.

How to use the game

- Divide your class into pairs A and B.

- Give all the As the cupboard 1 cards and all the Bs the recipe 1 cards.

- **The object of the game is for the Bs to find out what they have in the cupboard, and work out what they need to buy to make the recipe.**

- To do this, they will have to ask the As questions, 'Is there any flour? How much is there?' 'Are there any eggs? How many are there?' etc.

- By comparing the amounts in the cupboard with the amounts needed for the recipe they will know how much they need to get.

- They should complete the shopping list at the side of the recipe.

- When they have finished, you can repeat with the cupboard 2 cards and the recipe 2 cards, reversing roles this time.

Demonstration

Demonstrate what to do, by taking B's role.
Tell the class, 'I'm going to make an apple cake.'
Show them the recipe.
Write 'Shopping List' up on the board.
Ask the A students, 'Is there any flour in the cupboard?'
When they say, 'Yes', ask, 'How much is there?'
When they reply, look at your recipe. Say, 'Hmm. I need 500 grams.'
Do a sum on the board: 500 - 250 = 250.
Write 250 grams flour on the shopping list.
Ask the Bs to continue with the next item (*sugar*).

Classroom language

Here is a recipe.
Here is a picture of your cupboard.
You want to make Apple Cake/Cheese and Tomato Omelette.
Ask what is in the cupboard, like this.
I'm going to make Apple Cake. *(taking a recipe)*
What do I need to buy? *(write 'Shopping List' on the board)*
I need flour. Is there any flour in the cupboard? *(to the A students)*
Hmm. How much is there?
250 grams. I need 500 grams *(write up the sum and then write 250 grams flour on the list on the board)*
OK. Now you go on.
Work in pairs.
Ask, 'Is there any ...? How much is there?' or 'Are there any ...? How many are there?'

20 Collectors

Type of activity
small group; collecting

Function practised
asking for things

Structures
Have you got a (cup)?
Yes, I have/Sorry! No, I haven't.

Topic area
kitchen objects

Essential vocabulary
cup, saucer, plate, bowl, knife, fork, spoon, teaspoon, kettle, teapot, milk jug, sugar bowl, mixing bowl, cake tin, scales, wooden spoon

Materials and preparation

Mentally divide your class into groups of three or four.
Copy and cut up one set of cards for each group.
There is a pictorial Rules sheet for this game on page 111. Make copies for each group after making the changes that are noted there.

How to use the game

- Divide your class into groups of three or four.

- Give one set of cards to each group.

- For the groups of three, take out one group of cards (tea making, crockery, cutlery or cake making).

- They should shuffle the cards and deal them out equally. They may look at their cards.

- The object of the game is to collect one set of cards that go together: tea making, cutlery, crockery or cake making. (The complete set of items is shown in the corner of each card.)

- To do this, players will have to take it in turns to ask each other for the items, e.g. 'Have you got a cup?'

- If the player asked has the item, he must give it to the first player.

- Then it is the next player's turn.

- The winner is the first player to collect all four cards in a set.

Demonstration

Demonstrate how to play the game by playing the first round all together.
Get the groups to deal out and look at their cards.
Ask them to look at the pictures in the top right-hand corner (draw a diagram of the box).
Have they any that make a set?
Put them together in their hands.
Are any cards missing from the set? Which ones?
Name a player in each group to begin.
Get them to ask any other player in the group for one of the cards they need: 'Have you got a ...?'
Get the player to answer, 'Yes, I have' (and give the card) or 'No, I haven't.'
Then get the next player in the circle to ask, 'Have you got a ...?'

Classroom language

Here are some cards.
Deal them out. *(demonstrate)*
Everyone should have four cards. Have you all got four cards?
Look at your cards.
Look at the picture at the top corner. *(show or draw diagram)*
Have you got any the same?
Which ones? Put them together in your hand. *(demonstrate)*
Have you got all the cards in the set? Are some missing?
Which ones do you need?
X, Y, Z. *(name one student in each group)* You begin.
Ask someone for a card you need. Say, 'Have you got a ...?'
Have you got the card? If you've got the card, say, 'Yes, I have.' Give it to X, Y, Z.
If you haven't got the card, just say, 'Sorry! No, I haven't.'
Good. Now it's the next player's turn.
A, B, C. You go on.

21 The great shopping race

Type of activity
whole class; collecting

Function practised
asking for things

Structures
Have you got any (steak)?
Here you are.
plus (optional): *How much/many do you want?* and words for amounts and containers

Topic area
shops and shopping

Essential vocabulary
butcher, baker, chemist, supermarket, greengrocer, newsagent
plus six of the following (i.e. each student will only be required to use six of the following sets of words during the game, not all thirty-six!):
ham, steak, pork chops, chicken, leg of lamb, bacon
brown bread, rolls, cake, buns, jam tarts, white bread
toothpaste, soap, aspirin, plasters, shampoo, deodorant
butter, tea, coffee, milk, sugar, rice
apples, oranges, bananas, potatoes, peas, cauliflower
evening newspaper, sweets, magazine, chocolates, a bar of chocolate, cigarettes
plus (optional): *100, 200, 250, 500, grams, kilo, loaf, box, tube, bar, packet, bar, bottle, litre, bag, jar*

Materials and preparation

This game works best with a minimum of twelve students.
For twelve or more students:
Make one copy of each of the SHOP NAMES.
Make one copy of each of the SHOPPING LISTS.
Make one copy of each of the PRODUCT CARDS.
If you have fewer than twelve students:
Either put your class together with another class or divide the class into pairs. (If there is an odd one, make a group of three.) How many pairs/groups are there in total?
Copy that number of shop names.
Copy the same number of shopping lists, but delete the items which cannot be found in the shops you have chosen.
Copy only the relevant product cards for the shops you have chosen.

NOTE   With the shopping lists, if you want your class to practise *much* and *many* and containers as well as *have got* - for example the exchange:
  'Have you got any (coffee)?'
  'Yes. How much do you want?'
  'One (jar).'
- then leave the amounts on the list. If you think this is too difficult for your class and want them simply to practise:

'Have you got any ...?'
'Yes, here you are/No, I'm sorry, I haven't.'
- then cut the amounts off the lists, leaving simply the products.

How to use the game

- Divide your class into six groups (or into pairs if you have under twelve students).

- Seat each group round a table.

- Give each group a shop name. Get them to stand it on their table.

- Give each group the product cards for their shop.

- Give each group a shopping list.

- **The object of the game is for each group to obtain the products on their shopping list.**

- To do this, they must send out one person from their group **and no more than one person** to obtain the first item on the list from another shop.

- They should go to the right shop (or what they think is the right shop) and ask, 'Have you got any ...?' The shop assistant will hand over the appropriate product card (if they are in the right shop!). (Or, if you are playing the harder version, she will ask, 'How much/many do you want?' and wait for the reply, before handing over the product card.)

- When they have got the product, they can return to their table and the next person can go off in search of another item.

Demonstration
Demonstrate how to play by playing the first round (first item) with the whole class together.
Make sure each group knows that only one person can go shopping.
Get them to choose that person.
Make sure each group knows that they can only shop for the **first** item on their shopping list.
Get them to identify that item.
Make sure they know that they are to bring back the product.
Make sure they know what to say ('Have you got any ...?').
(If you are playing the harder version, make sure the shop assistants know to ask, 'How much/many do you want?' before handing over the product.)
Then say, 'Ready, steady, go!'
When they have all got back to their tables with the right card (check it is right!), make sure they know a different person is to go off for the next item.
Then let them race on to the end of the list.

Classroom language

Here is a shop sign. *(get them to put it on the table)*
Here are the things you sell in your shop. *(give them the right product cards for their shop)*
Here is a shopping list. *(give each group their list)*
You must go shopping and get the things on the list.
Choose one person to go shopping.
OK. Who is going in each group?
Look at your list. What is the first thing?
When I say 'Go', go to the right shop. Ask, 'Have you got any ...?'
Shop assistants: give them the picture and say, 'Here you are' (or ask, 'How much/many do you want?').
When you get the picture, come back to your table.
Are you ready? Ready, steady, go!
Have you got the right picture?
Good. Now it's the next person's turn.

22 Martian lotto

Type of activity
small group; matching

Function practised
describing appearances

Structures
Has he got (two square heads)?
He's got (two square heads).
He hasn't got (two square heads).

Topic area
people's (or aliens') appearances

Essential vocabulary
round, square, long, short, small, big, head, body, legs, arms, feet, hands; numbers

Materials and preparation

Mentally divide your class into groups of three or four. Copy a set of LOTTO BOARDS and a set of INDIVIDUAL CARDS for each group. (For groups of three, leave out one board and its matching cards.)
There is a pictorial Rules sheet for this game on page 106. Make copies for each group after making the changes that are noted there.

How to use the game

- Divide the class into groups of three or four.

- Give each group a set of boards and a pack of cards.

- They should take one board each and place the cards face down in a pile in the middle of the table.

- The first player should take a card from the pile and

look at it, without showing it to the others.

- She can make two statements about it, one beginning, 'He's got ...', the other beginning, 'He hasn't got ... .'

- The others can then ask questions: 'Has he got ...?'

- When one player thinks the card matches one of the aliens on his lotto board, he can ask to see it.

- If it does match, he can place it on his board and take the next card from the pile.

- **The object of the game is to find cards that match the four pictures on the lotto board.**

- The player to do so first is the winner.

Demonstration

Demonstrate how to play by playing the first round with the class as a whole.
Take one of the cards, and, holding it so they can't see it, make two statements about it.
Then invite questions from the class. Get them to look at the pictures on their lotto boards and prompt them to ask, 'Has he got ...?'
When a student or students thinks/think they have a matching picture, you can show them the card.
Then get them to go on in their groups.

Classroom language

Here are some boards.
Take one each.
Here are some cards.
Put them face down in the middle. *(demonstrate)*
I'm going to take a card. Listen carefully. 'He's got (three round heads). He hasn't got (four feet).'
Look at your boards. Have you got the same picture?
Ask me questions: 'Has he got ...?'
(answer their questions, then) Who has got the same picture?
X, Y, Z, you think you've got the same picture? Let's see.
(comparing pictures) Yes, they're the same. Good.
You can take the card and put it on your board, like this. *(demonstrate)*
Now, X, Y, Z. You take the next card from the pile.
Say two things: 'He's got ...' and 'He hasn't got ... .'
Now, play in your groups. Ask questions.

23 Airport convention

Type of activity
whole class; exchanging

Function practised
describing appearances

Structures
He's/She's/They've got (dark hair).
He's/She's/They're (tall).
He's/She's/They're wearing (shorts).

Topic area
appearances and clothes

Essential vocabulary
either: *dark/fair/curly/straight/long/short hair,*
tall, small, fat, thin, beard, glasses
or: *shorts, trousers, suit, jacket, shirt, skirt, dress, T-shirt,*
blouse, jumper, trainers, shoes, sandals
or both, depending on the needs of your class

Materials and preparation

There are enough cards for up to 32 students. If you have more than 32, play in two groups.
Mentally divide your class in half.
Select that number of MISSING PERSONS CARDS (1) and (2) and copy them twice.
Cut them up.
On one set, cut off the words. Leave them on the other set.

NOTES (1) If your students have already studied the order of adjectives, you can prompt them to use combinations such as. 'He has short, dark hair.' If they haven't, they can say, 'He has short hair. It is dark/He has dark hair.'

(2) If you want to practise *they* forms as well as *he* and *she*, allocate some students two similar cards (e.g. a man and woman who are both short and fat, or who both have dark hair).

How to use the game

- If you have more than 32 students, divide them into two groups; if not, play as a whole class.

- Divide the class into two halves A and B.

- Give the As a missing person card with words on (or two cards if you are practising *they* forms).

- Get them to stand up and come to the front.

- Tell them they are at an airport. They are supposed to meet the person/people on their card and take them to a conference (or they are meeting their aunt or uncle from abroad - choose the context that suits your students best). They don't know the person, but have this photo of them.

- Then give all the Bs a card (or two cards) without words.

- They can remain seated.
- Tell them they are at an airport. They are waiting for their flight, sitting in a café. The person in their card is standing somewhere near them looking lost.
- **The object of the game is for all the As to find the person they have come to meet.**
- To do this, they will have to stand up and move around the class, asking the Bs if they have seen the person they are looking for, and describing them (either their physical appearance or their clothes or both).
- When a B student hears the description of the card she is holding, she should give it to the A student.
- When they have finished, you can play again, reversing roles.

Demonstration

Demonstrate how to play the game by taking an A card and playing it yourself, while the class watch.
Go up to a B student and say, 'Excuse me. I'm looking for someone. *(describe the person on your card)* Have you seen her/him?'
Repeat with one or two more students.
Then explain that when they find their missing person, the B students should hand over the card. They can then sit down.

Classroom language

You are all in Group A.
You are all in Group B.
Group A, stand up and come to the front.
You are in an airport.
You are meeting someone.
Here is a photo of the person you must meet.
(giving out cards)
You don't know this person, but you must meet them and take them to a conference. (Or: This is your aunt/uncle. You don't know them because they live in Canada, but you have their photo.)
Group B, you are at the same airport.
You are sitting in a café.
This person is standing near you. *(give out the cards to the Bs)*
Group A, you must find your person.
Ask the Bs.
Like this. *(taking a card and going up to a B)* Excuse me. I'm looking for someone. Can you help me?
(describe the person on your card)
OK. Now you play. When you find your person, take the card and sit down.

24 Follow the yellow brick road

Type of activity
pairwork; information gap

Function practised
giving directions

Structures
imperatives: *turn, go, cross, take*
prepositions of movement and place: *along, on, over, round, in, into, across, beside, past, in the middle of, on top of*

Topic area
the countryside

Essential vocabulary
woods, lake, river, bridge, hill, mountain, island, road, treasure, clue, left, right, straight on, the first/second/third on the left/right

---

Materials and preparation

Mentally divide your class into pairs A and B.
Make copies of MAP A for all the As.
Make copies of MAP B for all the Bs.
Make one copy of the CLUE CARDS for each pair.
Cut these up and arrange them in piles facing downwards, so that the clues when turned up will be in order: 1-8.
Secure each set of clues with a paperclip.

How to use the game

- Divide your class into pairs A and B.
- Give map A to all the As.
- Give map B to all the Bs.
- They should not show the maps to each other.
- Give each pair a pile of clue cards.
- They should remove the paperclip and place the pile exactly as it is, face down, between them.
- Tell them they are about to go on a treasure hunt.
- The clues are in the pile in front of them.
- They should take turns to turn these up one at a time. Student A should begin.
- When they have traced the route given in the clue, they can turn up the next clue.
- Unfortunately, their maps are not complete, so they will have to ask each other for help, to find exactly where the clues are.
- **The object of the game is to find the treasure.**
- To do this, they will have to help each other to follow the clues until they come to the last one which will tell them where the treasure is (on the island!).

Demonstration

Demonstrate how to do this by getting all the As to turn up the first clue.

Tell the As to give the Bs directions to find the first clue.

(Make sure they do this by saying, 'Go straight on. Turn left/right' etc.)

Get them both to trace the route in on their maps. When they have all done this, get the Bs in each group to turn up the next card. Tell them to take turns.

The last clue will tell them where the treasure is.

Classroom language

You two work together: A and B, A and B. *(etc.)*
Here is a map.
Don't show it to your partner!
It's a treasure map. *(explain with a drawing)*
These are clues. They will help you find the treasure.
All the As, put up your hands.
Take the first clue.
Can you see Number 1 on your map?
Good. Tell your partner how to get there. 'Go straight on. Go past the road on the left. Clue 1 is on the ... beside the ... .'
Draw the way on the map like this. *(show with sketch of part of the map on the board)*
OK. Now, B. You take the next card. Tell A how to get there.

25 Dream tickets

Type of activity
whole class; exchanging

Function practised
asking about likes and dislikes

Structures
Do you like (cycling)?
Yes, I do. I love it!
No, I don't!
This is for you.

Topic area
hobbies

Essential vocabulary
cycling, walking, skiing, painting, football, tennis, gardening, sailing, playing the guitar, cooking, riding, climbing, prize, have won, free holiday, hobby

Materials and preparation

Copy one HOBBY CARD for every student.
Copy one HOLIDAY PRIZE CARD for every student.
Make sure the holidays match the hobbies you have

selected.
It would be a nice touch if you could put the holiday prizes in envelopes, as if they had really come through the post.

How to use the game

- Give each student one hobby card.

- Let them read it, then tell them they have won a prize! It's a free holiday!

- Give out the envelopes (making sure everyone gets a holiday that is nothing to do with his hobby!).

- Ask them if they are happy with the holiday.

- Ask them to get up and see if anyone else would like their holiday.

- **The object of the game is to give away the holiday you've got and get one that matches your hobby (card).**

- To do this, students will have to stand up and move around the class asking, 'Do you like ...?' until they find someone who has the hobby featured in their holiday.

- They can then give their holiday away.

- When they have given away the unwanted holiday and got a better one in exchange, they can sit down.

Demonstration

Demonstrate how to do this by taking an example hobby and holiday.

Tell them, for example, 'I like sailing. But this holiday is a gardening holiday!'

Go up to a student and ask, 'Do you like gardening?' When she says, 'No', look disappointed and try another student.

Tell the class, 'When you find someone who likes gardening, give them the holiday.'

When you have given your holiday to someone and got a holiday you like, sit down.

Classroom language

Here is a card.
This is your hobby.
You have won a holiday!
It's very exciting.
This is your prize.
Do you like your holiday? (Look at your hobby card.)
No? Well, maybe you can give your holiday to someone.
Stand up. Ask people, 'Do you like ...?'
Like this. Look. *(show card)* My hobby is sailing.
My prize is a **gardening** holiday. *(show prize; look fed up)*
Maybe I can find someone who likes gardening. *(going up to a student)* Do you like gardening?
No? Do you like gardening? *(trying another student)*

Now you try.
When you find someone who likes your holiday, give it to them. *(demonstrate)*
When you have given your holiday to someone and when you get a holiday you like, *(demonstrate 'give' and 'get')* sit down.

26 Lost tribes

Type of activity
whole class; combining

Function practised
asking about habits and lifestyles

Structures
Do you (eat fish)?
Yes, I do/No, I don't.

Topic area
daily life

Essential vocabulary
eat, drink, live in, like, move around, house, dancing, in the hills, beside the sea, in the country, tea, milk, beer, wine, wooden, straw, mud, tent, rice, corn, fish, cheese

Materials and preparation
Mentally divide your class by four.
Copy and cut up the resulting number of TRIBE CARDS.

How to use the game
- Give out the tribe cards at random so everyone has one each.

- Tell them there are four different tribes in the class.

- Their card tells them about the tribe.

- **The object of the game is to find the rest of their tribe.**

- To do this, they will have to stand up and move around the room asking, 'Do you (eat fish)?' etc. until they find the other people in their tribe.

- When they have found everyone, they should sit down together and make up a name for themselves.

- Get feedback from each group at the end - about their tribe's name and lifestyle.

Demonstration
Demonstrate how to play by taking a card yourself.
Read out what is on it to the class.
Tell them you must find other people who live like you.
Demonstrate, going up to two or three students and asking the questions, 'Do you eat/drink/live in/like ...?'
Then tell the class to continue like this.

When they have found the other people in their tribe, they should sit down and make up a name for themselves.

Classroom language
In this room there are four tribes.
Here is a card.
The card tells you what you eat, what you drink, how you live, what you like in your tribe.
In this room there are other people in the same tribe as you.
Find them!
Like this.
This is my card. *(read it out)*
I want to find the people in my tribe. *(demonstrate going up to a few students and asking 'Do you ...?' questions)*
When you find your tribe, stay together. *(show this with a gesture)*
When you find ... people, *(tell them how many in each tribe)* sit down together.
Talk about your tribe. What is your tribe's name?

27 Does it eat people?

Type of activity
pairwork; arranging

Function practised
asking about habits

Structures
Does it (fly)?
Yes, it does. No, it doesn't.

Topic area
animals

Essential vocabulary
eat, have, swim, fly, live, give, bite, jump, grass, meat, water, milk, wool

NOTE   The names of the animals are not actually essential for playing the game, but students will probably like to know them: *cat, dog, cow, sheep, duck, fish, frog, snake, kangaroo, crocodile, giraffe, tiger*

Materials and preparation
Make one copy of the ANIMAL BOARDS for every student in the class.
Leave half of them as picture boards and cut the other half up into cards.
Make copies of the NUMBER BOARD for half the class.

How to use the game

- Divide the class into pairs A and B.

- Give the As the cards and the number boards and the Bs the picture boards.

- The Bs should not show the As the pictures on the boards.

- The As should spread their cards on the table so they can see them all.

- **The object of the game is for the As to arrange their picture cards on the number board in the same order as on the Bs' board.**

- To do this, they will have to ask questions about each picture: 'Does it ...?' (e.g. 'Does it eat grass? Does it have four legs? Does it fly?') until they can guess which animal is next on the board.

Demonstration

Demonstrate how to do this, by only giving out the cards and number boards to begin with.
Get the pairs to spread them out on the desk so they can see all the cards.
Draw a plan of the number board on the blackboard.
Take an animal board yourself and show it to them very quickly (enough for them to see that there are pictures of animals, but too quickly for them to remember which ones go where).
Tell them you want them to guess which animal is in square 1 (show them on the blackboard diagram).
Prompt them to ask questions beginning with 'Does it ...?'
When they guess, get each A student to take that card and put it in position on their number board.
Then give out the picture boards to the Bs and get them to go on in pairs.

Classroom language

Here are some animal pictures.
Spread them out on the desk. *(demonstrate)*
Look at the board.
This is a drawing of your number board. *(show them)*
Here is a board with animal pictures. *(showing them very quickly)*
Can you guess which animal is in square 1? *(pointing to the board drawing)*
Ask me questions.
Ask questions with 'Does it ...?': 'Does it eat meat? Does it fly?' *(when they guess correctly)* 'Yes! It's a cat!'
Look at your pictures.
Find the cat.
Put it on square 1.
Good. Now here is a board for you.
Don't show it to your partner!
Play in pairs.
Guess the animal in square 2.
Ask questions with 'Does it ...?'

28 Jobmatch

Type of activity
whole class; matching

Function practised
asking about daily routines

Structures
When do you (get up)?
I (get up) at (five) o'clock.

Topic area
work routines

Essential vocabulary
get up, go to work, have lunch, come home, go to bed, postman, teacher, doctor, secretary, factory worker, nurse, farmer, singer

Materials and preparation

Mentally divide your class in half.
Select that number of JOB DESCRIPTION CARDS.
Copy each twice.
On one set, cut off and discard the words so that only the pictures remain.

How to use the game

- Divide your class in half.

- Give one half the pictures and give the other half the complete pictures and words.

- Ask the half with the pictures to stand up.

- Tell them that somewhere in the class (one of the students sitting down) is someone with the same job as each of them.

- **The object of the game is to find the person with the same job.**

- To do this, they will have to stand up and move around the class asking questions about daily routines: 'When do you get up/go to work/have lunch/come home/go to bed?' until they find someone they think has the same job. (They may not tell each other what the job is until they have asked all the questions.)

- When they find somone they think has the same job, they may show them their picture.

- If it is the same, they can sit down together.

- Ask them to talk about their job, e.g. 'Do you like your job?'

Demonstration

Demonstrate how to do this by taking a picture card yourself and going up to one of the students sitting down (choose someone with a different job).
Ask her the questions.
When she has answered all the questions, shake your

head and say, 'No, it's not the same job. You're not a
..., are you?'
Compare the two pictures and hold them up for the
class to see they're not the same.
Repeat with another student.
Then let the students carry on the game.
Tell them when they've found their person to sit down
together and talk about the question on the board (write
up: 'Do you like your job?').

Classroom language

X, Y, Z. *(naming students)* You are in Group A.
Come to the front.
The others - you are Group B.
Stay sitting down.
This is your job. *(handing out cards to Group B)*
This is your job. *(handing out cards to Group A)*
Group A, you must find someone in Group B with
the same job.
Ask questions, like this. *(demonstrate as above)*
OK. Now you do it.
Ask questions.
Remember, ask questions first. **Don't show your
picture and don't say the name of your job!**
When you have asked the questions, then you can
show your picture.
When you find your partner, sit down together.
Talk about the question on the board.
OK. Now begin.

29 World map

Type of activity
small group; quiz

Function practised
asking about lifestyles

Structures
Where does he/she live?
What does he/she wear?
What does he/she eat?
How does he/she travel?

Topic area
countries and customs

Essential vocabulary
tent, longhouse, (wooden) hut, flat, igloo, apartment, robe,
sari, sarong, cloak, kimono, jeans, fur coat, couscous, barley,
curry, rice, corn, hamburger, fish, by bicycle, on foot, by
camel, by subway, by moped, by car, by sled, by yaks
(Students do not need to know this vocabulary as all
words are given on the people cards.)

Materials and preparation

Mentally divide your class into groups of three or four.
Copy three WORLD MAPS and one set of PEOPLE CARDS
for each group.
There is a pictorial Rules sheet for this game on page
107. Make copies for each group.

How to use the game

- Divide your class into groups of three or four.

- Appoint (or ask the group to choose) one Quizmaster
  for each group.

- Give the Quizmaster a set of people cards to be
  placed face down in front of him.

- Give the others in the group a world map each.

- The Quizmaster takes the top card from the pile and
  looks at it, but does not show it to the others.

- He can tell the others, 'It's a man' or 'It's a woman.'

- The others can ask him questions, e.g. 'What kind of
  house does he live in? What does he/she eat? What
  does he/she wear? How does he/she travel?'

- **The object of the game is to guess the nationality
  of the person on the people card.**

- The player who guesses correctly takes the card and
  places it in the right place on their map.

- At the end the player with most cards on their map is
  the winner.

Demonstration
Demonstrate how to play the game by playing one
round with the class.
Draw a stick person on the board.
Write up the questions: 'Where does he/she live? What
does he/she eat and drink? What does he/she wear? How
does he/she travel?' on the board.
Get them to ask you.
Give the following answers: 'In a brick house.' 'Fish and
chips and beer.' 'A bowler hat, a raincoat and an
umbrella.' 'By car.' *(do quick sketches of all these on the
board)*
Ask them if they can guess which country he comes
from. (England!)
When they guess, get the Quizmaster in each group to
turn up the first card in the pile.
Get the groups to ask him the same questions.
Ask, 'Who guessed first?'
Get them to take the card and put it on their maps.
Then let them play on by themselves in their groups
(rub out the questions on the board).

Classroom language

Here are some maps. Take one each.
Here are some cards.
Put them face down in a pile.
Look at the board. *(draw the man and write the questions)*
Who is he? Ask me the questions.
Who can guess where he comes from?
Good! Now in each group choose one student.
OK. You take the first card **but don't show it to the others!**
The others, you ask questions. *(point to the questions on the board)*
Can you guess where he/she comes from?
Who guessed first?
Good. You can take the card and put it on the map.
OK. Take the next card and go on.

30 Lie detectors

Type of activity
small group; matching

Function practised
talking about habits and routines

Structures
How often do you (laugh)?
frequency adverbs: *once, never, often, sometimes, twice, every day/year/night/morning/week/weekend*
prepositions of time: *on, at*

Topic area
everyday activities

Essential vocabulary
laugh, cry, quarrel (with someone), do (some exercise), lie, read (a book), clean (the house), stay up (all night), drive (badly), drink (champagne), go (to the cinema), spend (too much money)

Materials and preparation

Mentally divide your class into groups of three or four.
Copy and cut up a set of ACTION CARDS and a set of FREQUENCY CARDS for each group.
There is a pictorial Rules sheet for this game on page 108. Make copies for each group after making the changes that are noted there.

NOTE For weaker students, leave the words on the cards. For more fluent students, cut off or tippex out the words before photocopying.

How to use the game

• Divide your class into groups of three or four.

• Give each group a set of action cards and a set of frequency cards.

• They should deal out the frequency cards and place the action cards face down in a pile in the middle.

• Player 1 should take an action card and ask the other players a question beginning with 'How often do you ...?', using the card as a cue, e.g. 'How often do you do some exercise?'

• The players must each reply, producing a frequency card, e.g. 'Never' or 'Once every five years.'

• Player 1 decides whose version is nearest the truth and gives the action card to that player.

• That player can lay down the action card and the frequency card.

• The next player in the circle takes an action card.

• **The object of the game is to get rid of all your cards.**

• The player who does so first is the winner.

Demonstration
Demonstrate how to play by getting all groups to play the first round together.
Get them to deal out the frequency cards and lay the action cards in the middle.
Get them to decide who is to begin.
Get that player in each group to turn up the first card and ask a question beginning, 'How often do you ...?'
Get all the other players to choose a frequency card and answer the question using that card.
Ask Player 1, 'Who is telling the truth?'
Get him to give the card to that player.
Get the player to put the action card and the frequency card down.

Classroom language

Here are some cards. *(give each group the frequency cards)*
Deal out these cards. *(demonstrate)*
Put these cards face down in the middle. *(give the action cards and demonstrate)*
Choose one student to begin.
Pick up a card from the pile. *(demonstrate)*
Look at it.
Ask a question. Begin: 'How often do you ...?'
The others: you must all answer.
Look at your cards.
Choose one. Now answer with the card 'Every day' or 'Once a week' etc.
Now, X, Y, Z. *(addressing Player 1 in each group)*
Which answer is true?
Give the card to the best answer. *(demonstrate)*
Good. You can throw away the cards.
Now you take the next card.

31 Talent scouts

Type of activity
pairwork; arranging

Function practised
asking about abilities

Structures
Can he/she (cook)?

Topic area
abilities and skills

Essential vocabulary
cook, climb, make people well, drive, sail, look after animals, sing, play the guitar, type, fly a plane, build, dance

Materials and preparation

Make one copy of the JOB BOARD for every student in the class.
Leave half of these as picture boards and cut the others up into cards.
Copy the number board from *Game 27 Does it eat people?* for half the class.

How to use the game

- Divide the class into pairs A and B.

- Give the As the cards and the number boards and the Bs the picture boards.

- The Bs should not show the As the pictures on the boards.

- The As should spread their cards on the table so they can see them all.

- **The object of the game is for the As to arrange their picture cards on the number board in the same order as on the Bs' board.**

- To do this, they will have to ask questions about each picture beginning, 'Can he/she ...?' ('Can he fly a plane? Can he drive?' etc.) until they can guess which job is next on the board.

Demonstration

Demonstrate how to do this, by only giving out the cards and number boards to begin with.
Get the pairs to spread them out on the desk so they can see all the cards.
Draw a plan of the number board on the classroom board.
Take a job board yourself and show it to them very quickly (enough for them to see that there are pictures, but too quickly for them to remember which ones go where).
Tell them you want them to guess which job is in square 1 (show them the diagram on the classroom board).
Prompt them to ask questions beginning with, 'Can he ...?'
When they guess, get each A student to take that card

and put it in position on their number board.
Then give out the picture boards to the Bs and get them to go on in pairs.

Classroom language

Here are some job pictures.
Spread them out on the desk. *(demonstrate)*
Look at the (classroom) board.
This is a drawing of your number board. *(show them)*
Here is a board with job pictures. *(showing them very quickly)*
Can you guess which job is in square 1? *(pointing to the drawing on the classroom board)*
Ask me questions.
Ask questions with 'Can', e.g. 'Can he fly a plane?' 'Can she make people well?'
(when they guess correctly) 'Yes! He's a dancer!'
Look at your pictures.
Find the dancer.
Put it on square 1.
Good. Now here is a board for you. **Don't show it to your partner!**
Play in pairs.
Guess the job in square 2.
Ask questions with 'Can'.

32 Room service

Type of activity
small group; matching

Function practised
making requests

Structures
Can I have a (blanket)/some (towels)/some (soap), please?

Topic area
hotel services

Essential vocabulary
towels, writing paper, blanket, pillow, soap, iron, hairdryer, cup of coffee, cold drink, pizza, cot, shampoo, aspirin, plasters, hot water, breakfast

Materials and preparation

Mentally divide your class into groups of three or four.
Make one copy of the SITUATION CARDS and two copies of the OBJECT CARDS for each group and cut them up.
There is a pictorial Rules sheet for this game on page 108. Make copies for each group after making the changes that are noted there.

How to use the game

- Divide your class into groups of three or four.

- Give each group a pack of object cards (two sets of cards).

- They should shuffle these together and deal them all out.

- Players can look at their hands.

- Give them the situation cards.

- They should place these face down in a pile in the middle.

- Player 1 begins by picking up the first situation card and looking at it.

- She should imagine she is in a hotel (Room 101) and makes a request to Room Service based on the situation on the card, e.g. if the situation is 'There isn't any soap', she should pretend to ring Room Service and ask, 'This is Room 101. Can I have some soap, please?'

- The other players should look at their cards.

- The first player to give her what she wants can throw away his object card.

- Then it is that player's turn to pick up the next situation card.

- **The object of the game is to get rid of all your cards.**

- The player who does so first is the winner.

Demonstration

Demonstrate how to play by getting everyone to play the first round together.

First of all, pick up a card yourself and make a request. Tell them you are in a hotel, and act out the situation for them (e.g. if the situation is 'There isn't any soap', act out going to wash your hands and looking for the soap). Say, 'Oh no, there isn't any soap. I'd better ring Room Service.' Act out dialling and speaking on the phone: 'This is Room 101. Can I have some soap, please?'

Then ask the students, 'Who can help me? Who has got some soap?'

Then play the first round together.

Name one student in each group to begin.

Get them to pick up their situation card and make a request beginning, 'This is Room 101. Can I have ..., please?'

Get the other students to look through their cards. Demonstrate that the first one to produce the item can throw his object card away and is the next to pick up a situation card from the pile.

Classroom language

Here are some cards.
Shuffle them. *(demonstrate)*
Deal them out. *(demonstrate)*
You can look at them.

Put these cards in a pile in the middle. *(demonstrate)*
Listen carefully. I'm in a hotel. *(pick up a situation card and read it, acting out the situation)*
I'd better phone Room Service. *(mime phoning and making your request)* This is Room 101. Can I have ..., please?
(asking students) Can anyone help me? Look at your cards.
Good. Now you do it.
X, Y, Z. *(naming students)* Take the first card.
Phone Room Service. Ask, 'Can I have ...?'
Who can help them?
Who was the first?
You can throw away your card. *(demonstrate)*
Good. Now it's your turn. Pick up a card. *(etc.)*

33 The restaurant game

Type of activity
small group; collecting

Function practised
asking for things

Structures
I'd like (tomato soup), please.
Certainly, sir/madam. Sorry, sir/madam, it's off.

Topic area
food

Essential vocabulary
soup, starter, main course, dessert, tomato, chicken, vegetable, peas, prawn cocktail, avocado, grapefruit, melon, fish and chips, sausage and beans, chicken pie and chips, cheese salad, apple pie, chocolate pudding, ice cream, fruit salad

Materials and preparation

Mentally divide your class into groups of three or four.
For the groups of four:
Copy one MENU CARD and one set of FOOD CARDS for each group.
For the groups of three:
Make one copy of the menu card.
Tippex out or delete one item in each section.
Then use this as your master to make a copy per group.
Make one copy of the cards for each group, but remember to remove the pictures of the items you have taken off the menu!
There is a pictorial Rules sheet for this game on page 111. Make copies for each group after making the changes that are noted there.

How to use the game

- Divide the class into groups of three or four.

- Give each group a menu and let them read it.

- Ask them each to decide on a four-course meal (soup, starter, main course and dessert) but not to tell the others. (They should write it down on a piece of paper.)

- Give the groups their food cards and ask them to deal these out.

- **The object of the game is to get four cards representing a four-course meal.**

- To do this, players will have to ask each other for items.

- Player 1 begins. He can ask any other player, 'I'd like ..., please.'

- If the player has the card, she **must** give it, saying, 'Certainly, sir/madam. Here you are.' If not, she should say, 'Sorry, sir/madam, it's off.'

- Then it's the next player's turn.

- The first player to get the menu he wants is the winner.

Demonstration

Demonstrate how to play by taking a hand of cards yourself.
Write up the menu you've chosen on the board.
Stand with one group and ask one of the players for one of your items: 'I'd like ..., please.'
Prompt her to say 'Certainly, sir/madam' and hand the card over if she has it or 'Sorry, sir/madam, it's off' if she hasn't.
Get another student in the group to ask one of the players for an item, while the class listens.
Then let them play on their own.
Tell them to call 'Finished' when the first player gets her menu.

34 Blind date

Type of activity
whole class; matching

Function practised
inviting, accepting and refusing

Structures
Would you like to (go to the cinema)?
I'd love to!
I'm sorry, I can't. I'm not free that day.

Topic area
social life and entertainment

Essential vocabulary
cinema, picnic, swimming, party, disco, theatre, skating

Materials and preparation

Mentally divide your class in half. If there is an odd number, ask one student to work with another one.
Make two copies of each DIARY for that number.
Keep them in two sets.

How to use the game

- Ask half the students to stand up. Give them each a diary page from one set of diaries.

- Give a diary page each, from the other set, to the other half who are seated.

- Tell them this is their diary for next week.

- They have one free day.

- They would like to go out on that day, but they would like a friend to go too.

- **The object of the game is to find someone to go out with them.**

- To do this, the students who are standing up will have to move around the room, asking the seated students, 'Would you like to ... on ...?' until they find someone to go with.

- Then they should sit down together.

Demonstration

Demonstrate how to do this by taking a diary yourself and going up to a couple of (seated) students and asking, 'Would you like to come to (a/the) ... on ...?' Prompt them to answer, 'Yes, I'd love to' or 'Sorry, I'm not free' or 'Sorry, I can't. I'm on holiday/away in London.'
Then get them to carry on.

Classroom language

Here is a diary.
Stand up, please/Stay sitting down, please.
This is your diary for next week.
You are only free on one day.
You want to go out that day.
But you don't want to go on your own.
You want to go with a friend.
Find a friend.
Like this. *(demonstrate asking a couple of students as above)*
Now you do it.
Look for a friend.
Ask, 'Would you like to ...?'
Answer, 'I'd love to!' or 'I'm sorry, I can't.'
When you find a friend, sit down with them.
Ready?
OK. Off you go!

35 Noises off

Type of activity
pairwork; guessing

Function practised
asking about what's happening

Structures
Are you (writing a letter)?
Yes, I am/No, I'm not.

Topic area
everyday actions

Essential vocabulary
writing, eating spaghetti, drinking, sleeping, driving, swimming, playing tennis, playing the trumpet, running, watching football, crying, reading a funny book, knitting

Materials and preparation

Mentally divide your class into pairs.
Copy and cut up one set of ACTIVITY CARDS per pair.

How to use the game

• Divide the class into pairs.

• Ask each pair to turn their chairs so they are back-to-back.

• Put a pile of cards face down on the desk where they can both reach it.

• They should take it in turns to pick up a card from the pile and mime the action on it, making the appropriate noise.

• **The object of the game is to try to guess the actions from the noise.**

• Their partner cannot see the mime but must try to guess the action from the noise, asking, 'Are you ... -ing ...?'

• If he cannot guess after three goes, he is allowed to look at the mime and guess again.

• Then it is his turn to pick up a card and mime with sound effects.

Demonstration

Demonstrate how to play by asking the class to close their eyes.
Mime opening a squeaky door, making the appropriate noise.
Ask them to guess what you are doing.
Prompt them to ask, 'Are you ... -ing ...?'
If they cannot guess, get them to open their eyes and watch your mime.
Then give them the cards and get them to carry on in pairs.

Classroom language

Close your eyes.
No looking!
Listen. *(make noise of creaky door)*
What am I doing?
Can you guess?
Ask, 'Are you ... -ing ...?' (e.g. 'Are you writing a letter?', 'Are you sleeping?')
Now open your eyes.
Watch. *(mime opening door with sound effect)*
Now can you guess?
Ask me, 'Are you ... -ing ...?'
Good. Now you play together.
Turn your chairs back-to-back, like this. *(demonstrate)*
Here are some cards.
Put them on the desk.
Who's going to begin?
Take a card.
Look at it.
Make a noise.
Can you guess? Ask, 'Are you ... -ing ...?'
You can have three guesses.
Then you can look!

36 Homelife

Type of activity
small group; matching

Function practised
asking what's happening

Structures
Is he/she (phoning)?
Yes, he/she is/No, he/she isn't.
Are they (eating)?
Yes, they are/No, they aren't.

Topic area
everyday actions

Essential vocabulary
phoning, opening (the door), going upstairs, coming in, eating, cooking, throwing (a ball), washing up, sitting down/reading (a book), watching (TV), playing cards, drinking (tea), digging, running, sleeping, picking flowers

Materials and preparation

Mentally divide your class into groups of three or four. Copy two sets of PICTURE BOARDS for each group. Cut up one set as boards and cut up the other set into individual picture cards. (For groups of three, you will need only three boards and their corresponding cards.) There is a pictorial Rules sheet for this game on page 106. Make copies for each group after making the changes that are noted there.

How to use the game

• Divide the class into groups of three or four.

• Give each group a set of boards and a pack of picture cards.

• They should take one board each and place the cards face down in a pile in the middle of the table.

• The first player should take a card from the pile and look at it, without showing it to the others.

• He can tell the others, 'He', 'She' or 'They'.

• The others try to guess what the picture is, by asking questions, 'Is he/she ... -ing ...?' or 'Are they ... -ing ...?'

• When one player thinks the card matches one of the actions on her board, she can ask to see it.

• If it does match, she can place it on her board and take the next card from the pile. If it doesn't match, the others go on guessing.

• **The object of the game is to find picture cards that match the four pictures on the board.**

• The player to do so first is the winner.

Demonstration
Demonstrate how to play by playing the first round with the class as a whole.

Take one of the cards, and, holding it so they can't see it, say to them, 'He' or 'She' or 'They'.
Then invite questions from the class. Get them to look at the pictures on their boards and prompt them to ask, 'Is he/she ... -ing ...?' or 'Are they ... -ing ...?'
When a student thinks they have a matching picture, you can show them the card.
Then get them to go on in their groups.

Classroom language

Here are some boards.
Take one each.
Here are some cards.
Put them face down in the middle. *(demonstrate)*
I'm going to take a card.
The person on the card is a 'he'.
Look at your boards. Have you got the same picture?
Ask me questions, 'Is he ... -ing ...?'
(answer their questions, then) Who has got the same picture?
X, Y, Z, you think you've got the same picture?
Let's see.
(showing picture) Yes, it's the same. Good.
You can take the card and put it on your board, like this. *(demonstrate)*
Now, X, Y, Z. You take the next card from the pile. Tell them, 'He', 'She' or 'They'.
Now, play in your groups. Ask questions.

37 In the park

Type of activity
pairwork; information gap

Function practised
describing what's happening

Structures
What's he/she doing?
What are they doing?
He's/She's/They're (walking).

Topic area
outdoor activities

Essential vocabulary
walking, reading (a newspaper/the menu), smoking a pipe, throwing (a ball/a toy), eating (bread/ice cream), pushing (a pram), climbing (a tree), sailing, playing the guitar, drinking (coffee), phoning, knitting, writing, chasing (a cat), swimming, running, sleeping, having a picnic

Materials and preparation

Make enough copies of PARK SCENE A for half your class and enough copies of PARK SCENE B for the other half.

How to use the game

- Divide your class into pairs A and B.

- Give park scene A to all the As and park scene B to all the Bs.

- They should not show their pictures to each other.

- **The object of the game is to find as many differences as possible between the two pictures.**

- To do this, they will have to describe their pictures to each other and make a note of the differences they find.

- There are ten differences.

Demonstration

Demonstrate how to play the game by taking park scene A yourself and asking the Bs to look at their pictures. Describe what's happening on the right of the picture ('A woman is walking and an old man is sitting on a bench and smoking a pipe').
Wait for them to protest, then ask them what's happening in their picture.
Write the heading on the board: 'Differences'.
Under it, write

	A	B
OLD MAN	smoking a pipe	reading a newspaper

Then get them to go on in pairs.

Classroom language

Work in pairs.
X and Y work together, A and B work together.
(etc.)
Here is a picture. **Don't show it to anyone!**
You both have pictures of a park. But there are some differences.
Find the differences.
Like this. (taking park scene A)
Listen carefully. I'm going to tell you about the picture.
On the right of my picture, a woman is walking and an old man is sitting on a bench. He is smoking a pipe.
What have you got in your picture?
And the As? What have you got in your picture?
OK. Work in pairs now.
Find more differences.
Write them down, like this. (writing on board)
How many differences can you find?

38 Eyewitnesses

Type of activity
whole class/small group

Function practised
asking about and describing past events

Structures
was and *were*

Topic area
houses

Essential vocabulary
kitchen, dining room, living room, hall, garden, body, murder, murderer

Materials and preparation

For 8-11 students:
Make one copy of the HOUSE PLAN and the list of PEOPLE.
Copy a ROLE CARD for every student.
When selecting role cards, make sure there are at least two people in every room so everyone has an eyewitness.
For 12 students:
Make one copy of the house plan for every student.
Copy a role card for every student.
For 13-23 students:
Make one copy of the house plan for every student.
Copy a role card for 12 students.
Add one or more POLICE OFFICER CARDS to make up the numbers.
For 24+ students:
Play in two groups.

How to use the game

- Give every student a house plan.

- Tell them a murder was committed last night at 11 o'clock.

- The body was found in the garden (X marks the spot).

- They were all in the house - their names are on the list of people beside the house plan.

- Give them a role card each.

- **The object of the game is to find out who did the murder.**

- To do this, they will have to find out where everyone was at 11 o'clock.

- They should stand up and move around the class asking everybody where they were at 11 o'clock.

- When they find out, they should write the names on the plan.

- Give them about five to ten minutes to do this, then ask them to get together in threes or fours.

- They should check their plans with each other and pool their information to find who the murderer was. Who isn't there? Who has left the house? (JANE)

Demonstration

Demonstrate how to do this by drawing a house plan on the board.
Go to one student and ask, 'What's your name? Where were you at 11 o'clock? Who was with you?'
Write the names in on the plan as she tells you.
Then ask them all to stand up and go on asking people and writing names.

Classroom language

Here is a plan of a house. *(give out the plan, then draw it on the board)*
There was a murder last night at 11 o'clock.
The body was here. *(draw X in)*
This is a list of names.
These people were all in the house.
You are one of these people. This is your name. *(giving out role cards)*
You must ask everybody where they were last night at 11 o'clock.
Like this.
What's your name? *(asking a student)*
Where were you at 11 o'clock?
Who was with you?
Now write the names on your plan, like this. *(writing in names on the board)*
Now you go on.
Stand up.
Ask questions.
Write the names on the plan.

OK, everyone. Sit down now.
Work with the people next to you.
Make a group of three or four.
Talk about your house.
Have you got the same names in the same rooms?
Look at the list of names. Who isn't in the house?
So, who did the murder?

39 Last night

Type of activity
small group; guessing

Function practised
asking about past events

Structures
Did you (go to a film) last night?
Yes, I did/No, I didn't.

Topic area
entertainment and leisure

Essential vocabulary
go to the cinema, read a book, go to bed early, go to a party, watch TV, write letters, go out for a meal, go to a café, do your homework, go to a play, go to a concert, go to a disco, go for a walk, see your friends

Materials and preparation

Mentally divide your class into groups of three or four.
Copy and cut up one set of ENTERTAINMENT CARDS per group.
There is a pictorial Rules sheet for this game on page 110. Make copies for each group after making the changes that are noted there.

How to use the game

- Divide your class into groups of three or four.

- Give each group a set of entertainment cards.

- Put the cards in a pile face down on the desk.

- They should take it in turns to pick up a card from the pile.

- The card shows what they did last night.

- They should not show it to the others.

- **The object of the game is to try to guess what the player holding the card did last night.**

- The other players must ask questions: 'Did you ...?' until they guess correctly.

- Then it is the turn of the player who guesses correctly to pick up a card.

Demonstration

Demonstrate how to play by picking up a card and asking the class, 'Guess what I did last night.'
Prompt them to ask, 'Did you ...?'
Answer, 'Yes, I did' or 'No, I didn't.'
When they guess, name a student in each group to take the first card from their pile.
Get them to carry on in groups.

(pick up a card) What did I do last night?
Can you guess?
Ask me, 'Did you ...?'
(when they have guessed)
Here are some cards.
Put them on the desk.
Who's going to begin?
X, Y, Z, take a card.
Look at it **but don't show it to the others!**
Can you guess? Ask, 'Did you ...?'
OK. Off you go.

40 Souvenir shopping

Type of activity
small group; matching

Function practised
talking about past events

Structures
I saw (a temple).
I went (walking/to the theatre).
I ate (rice).
I drank (tea).
Did you buy (this) there?

Topic area
holidays

Essential vocabulary
walking, dancing, cycling, swimming, sailing, theatre, museum, tea, beer, wine, rice, hamburger, coke, spaghetti, salad, fish and chips, sandwiches, sausages, mountains, rain, TV
(more unusual vocabulary is given on the holiday snaps cards: *paella, sherry, desert, tacos, margaritas, moussaka, ouzo, Chianti, castle, snails, skyscrapers, diner, temple, pagoda, sake, tulips, windmills, fondue*)
(It is not necessary to know the names of the souvenirs in order to play the game.)

Materials and preparation
Mentally divide your class into groups of three or four.
Make one copy of the SOUVENIR CARDS and one copy of the HOLIDAY SNAPS CARDS for each group.
There is a pictorial Rules sheet for this game on page 108. Make copies for each group after making the changes that are noted there.

How to use the game
- Divide your class into groups of three or four.
- Give each group a set of souvenir cards.
- They should deal these out.
- They can look at their cards.
- Give each group a pile of holiday snaps cards.
- They should place these face down in a pile on the desk.
- One student should take the first holiday snaps card and look at it, without showing the others.
- He can tell the others four things about his holiday: 'I saw ..., I ate ..., I drank ..., I went ... .'
- The others should guess where he went.
- If a student has the appropriate souvenir card in her hand, she can hand it to him saying, 'Did you buy (this) there?'
- **The object of the game is to match the holiday snaps with the souvenirs.**
- The player who gets rid of all their cards first is the winner.

Demonstration
Demonstrate how to play by taking one holiday snap yourself and saying four things about it, e.g. 'I saw some castles, I ate paella, and I drank sherry and I went swimming.'
Ask, 'Where did I go on holiday?'
Then: 'I bought a souvenir there. Has anyone got it?'
Get the student(s) producing the card to ask, 'Did you buy this there?'
Then get them to go on in their groups.

Classroom language
Here are some souvenir cards.
Deal them out. *(demonstrate)*
You can look at your cards.
Here are some holiday snaps cards.
Put them face down in the middle. *(demonstrate)*
Listen. I've got a holiday snaps card. *(taking a card)*
I'm going to tell you about my holiday, e.g. 'I saw a castle, I ate paella, and I drank sherry and I went swimming.'
Where did I go on holiday?
Spain!
I bought a souvenir there. Has anyone got it?
Ask, 'Did you buy (this) there?'
Yes! I did!
OK. Now you play.
Who is going to begin?
Right. Take the first card.
Say four things about your holiday: 'I saw ..., I ate ..., I drank ..., I went ... .'
Good. Now you go on.

Beginners'
COMMUNICATION
Games

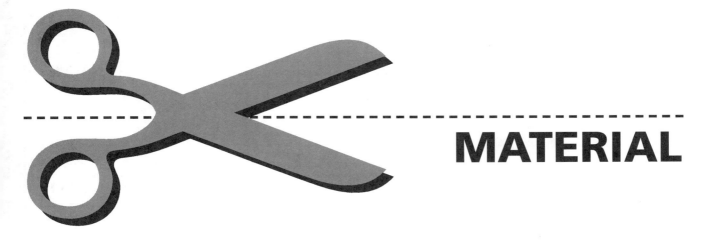

MATERIAL

1 Doppelganger

NAME CARDS

Peter	Sue	Rob	Beth	Mark
Jane	Tim	Anna	John	Mary
Dan	Pat	Ben	Kate	Adam
Alice	Jack	Claire	Sam	Jess
Peter	Sue	Rob	Beth	Mark
Jane	Tim	Anna	John	Mary
Dan	Pat	Ben	Kate	Adam
Alice	Jack	Claire	Sam	Jess

2 Spelling lotto (1)

WORD CARDS

table	chair	house	book
pen	girl	boy	man
dog	fish	zoo	jam
television	queen	X-ray	window

2 Spelling lotto (2)

LOTTO BOARDS

table   chair

book   pen

house   television

girl   queen

boy   man

fish   zoo

dog   X-ray

jam   window

3 Ladybird bingo (1)

LOTTO BOARDS

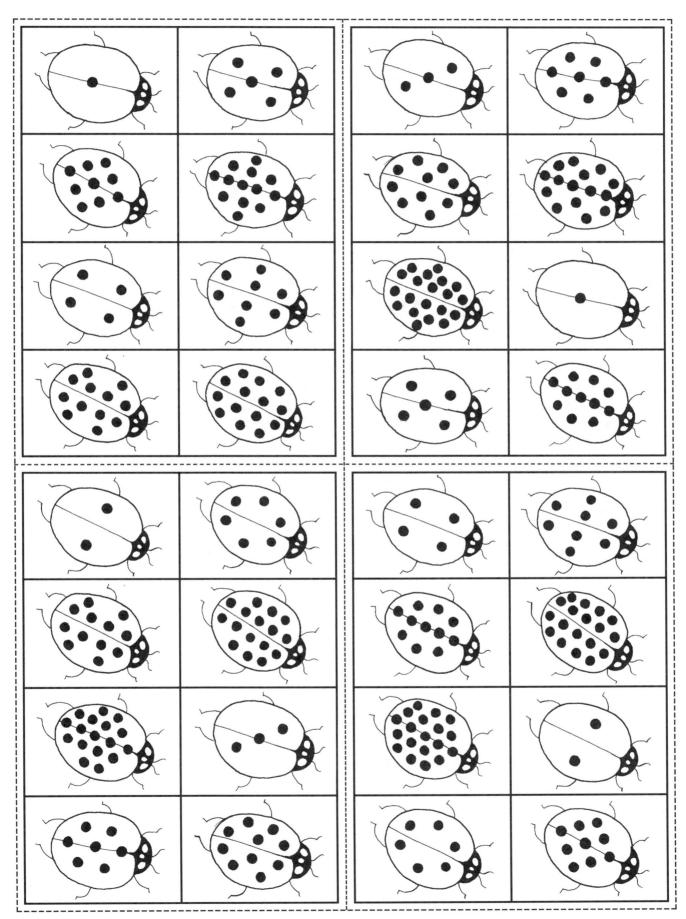

3 Ladybird bingo (2)

CARDS

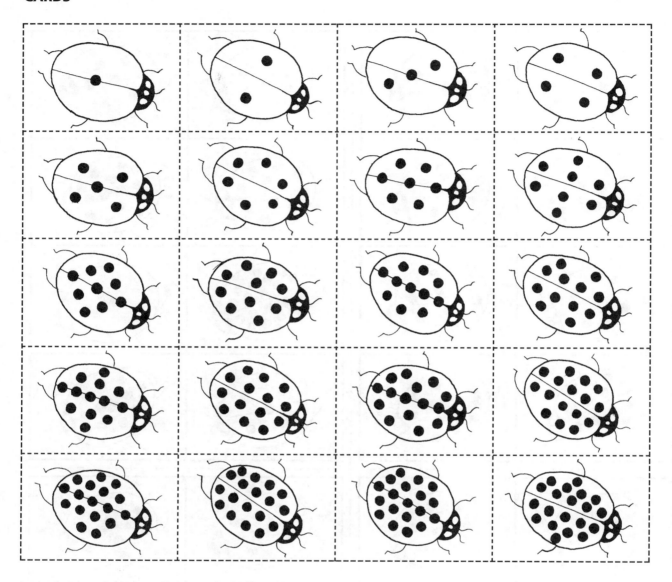

4 Clockmatch

CLOCK CARDS

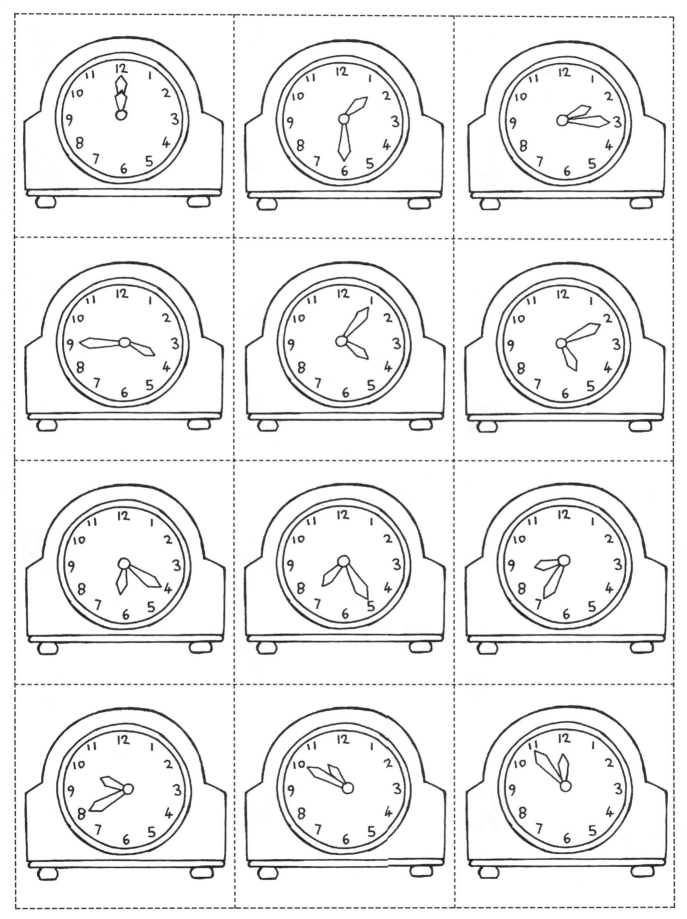

5 Lost in the post (1)

LETTER CARDS

Mr Sam Green 15 Main Street NEWTOWN	**Mr Sam Green 15 High Street NEWTOWN**	Mrs Sue Green 24 Main Street NEWTOWN
Mrs Sue Green 23 Main Street NEWTOWN	Mr Sam Black 30 High Street NEWTOWN	**Mr Sam Black 30 Main Street NEWTOWN**
Mrs Sue Black 42 Main Street NEWTOWN	**Mrs Sue Black 42 High Street NEWTOWN**	Mr Sam Brown 12 Main Street NEWTOWN
Mr Sam Brown 12 High Street NEWTOWN	Ms Sue Brown 16 Main Street NEWTOWN	**Miss Sue Brown 14 High Street NEWTOWN**
Mr Sam Blue 22 Main Street NEWTOWN	**Mr Sam Blue 28 Main Street NEWTOWN**	Miss Sue Blue 28 High Street NEWTOWN
Ms Sue Blue 27 Main Street NEWTOWN	Mr Sam Grey 1 High Street NEWTOWN	**Mr Sam Grey 1 Main Street NEWTOWN**
Mrs Sue Grey 5 High Street NEWTOWN	**Mrs Sue Grey 5 Main Street NEWTOWN**	

5 Lost in the post (2)

NAME CARDS

NAME Mr Sam Green ADDRESS 15 Main Street NEWTOWN	NAME Mr Sam Green ADDRESS 15 High Street NEWTOWN	NAME Mrs Sue Green ADDRESS 24 Main Street NEWTOWN
NAME Mrs Sue Green ADDRESS 23 Main Street NEWTOWN	NAME Mr Sam Black ADDRESS 30 High Street NEWTOWN	NAME Mr Sam Black ADDRESS 30 Main Street NEWTOWN
NAME Mrs Sue Black ADDRESS 42 Main Street NEWTOWN	NAME Mrs Sue Black ADDRESS 42 High Street NEWTOWN	NAME Mr Sam Brown ADDRESS 12 Main Street NEWTOWN
NAME Mr Sam Brown ADDRESS 12 High Street NEWTOWN	NAME Ms Sue Brown ADDRESS 16 Main Street NEWTOWN	NAME Miss Sue Brown ADDRESS 14 High Street NEWTOWN
NAME Mr Sam Blue ADDRESS 22 Main Street NEWTOWN	NAME Mr Sam Blue ADDRESS 28 Main Street NEWTOWN	NAME Miss Sue Blue ADDRESS 28 High Street NEWTOWN
NAME Ms Sue Blue ADDRESS 27 Main Street NEWTOWN	NAME Mr Sam Grey ADDRESS 1 High Street NEWTOWN	NAME Mr Sam Grey ADDRESS 1 Main Street NEWTOWN
NAME Mrs Sue Grey ADDRESS 5 High Street NEWTOWN	NAME Mrs Sue Grey ADDRESS 5 Main Street NEWTOWN	

6 Wedding photos (1)

WEDDING PHOTO

6 Wedding photos (2)
FAMILY TREE CARDS

FAMILY TREE A
BRIDE'S FAMILY

Joe — Elsie

Jess — Tom   Pete — Sue

Sam   Ann   ME   Mike

FAMILY TREE B
GROOM'S FAMILY

Jim — Betty

Jane — Al   Ben — Liz

Tim   Beth   ME   John

7 Mine! (1)

FAMILY CARDS

7 Mine! (2)

CLOTHES CARDS

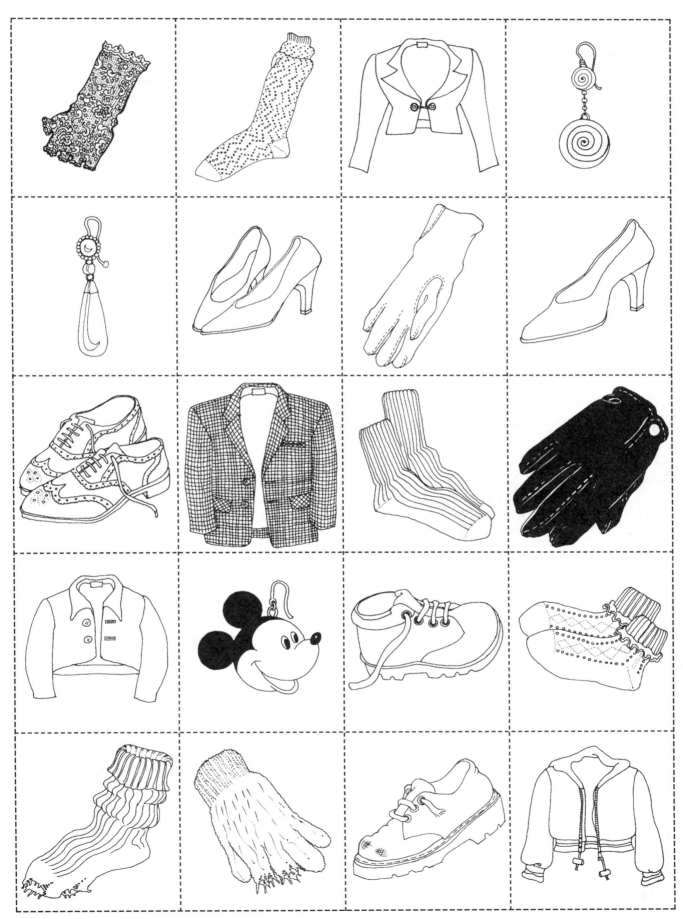

8 National dress (1)

COUNTRY CARDS

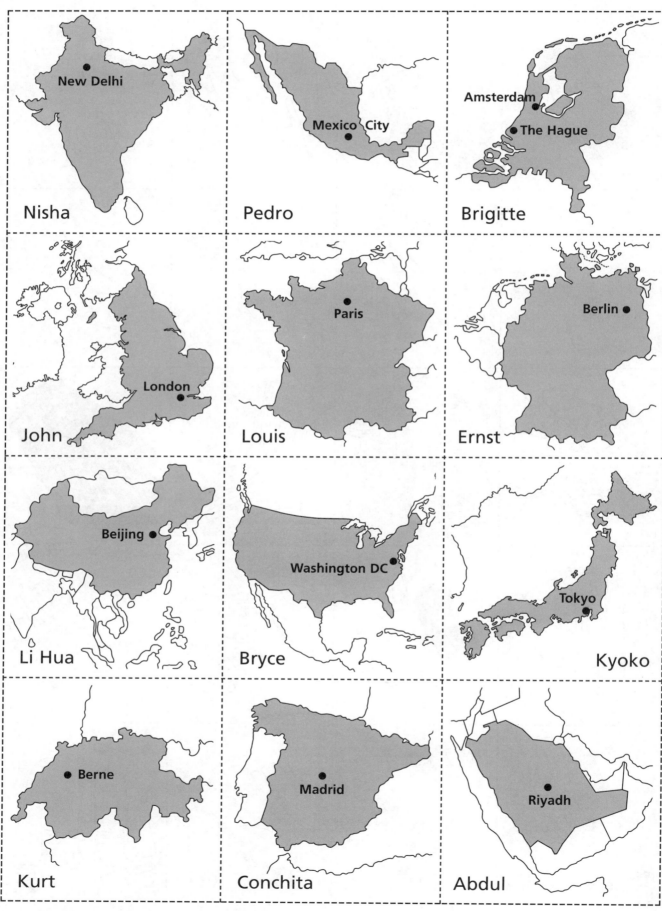

Nisha

Pedro

Brigitte

John

Louis

Ernst

Li Hua

Bryce

Kyoko

Kurt

Conchita

Abdul

8 National dress (2)

DRESS CARDS

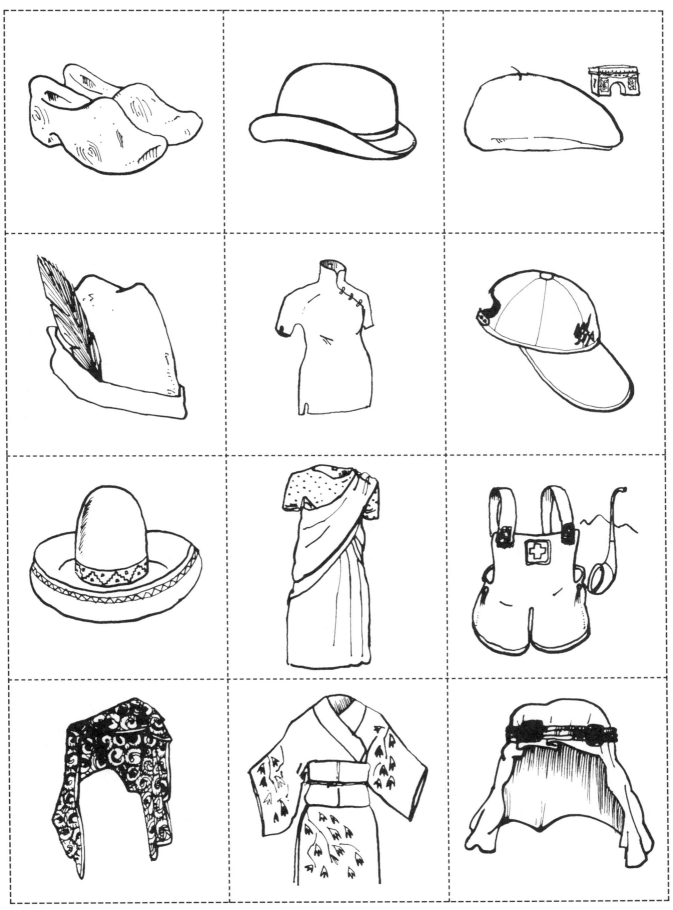

16 Packing

ROOM **A**

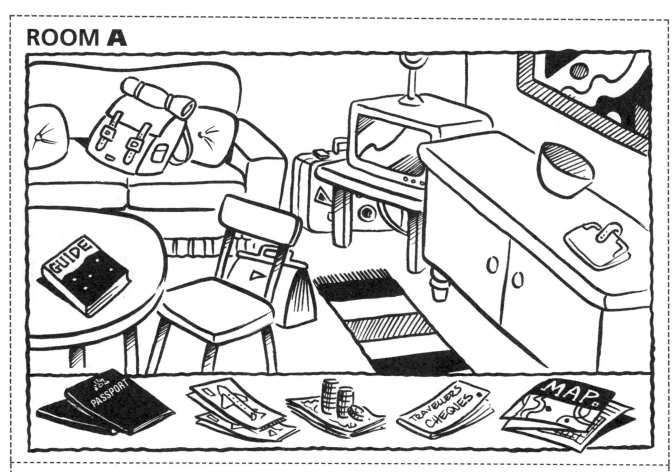

ROOM **B**

17 Something old, something new (1)

OLD LIVING ROOM

NEW LIVING ROOM

17 Something old, something new (2)

OLD BEDROOM

NEW BEDROOM

18 My home town (1)

TOWN PLANS

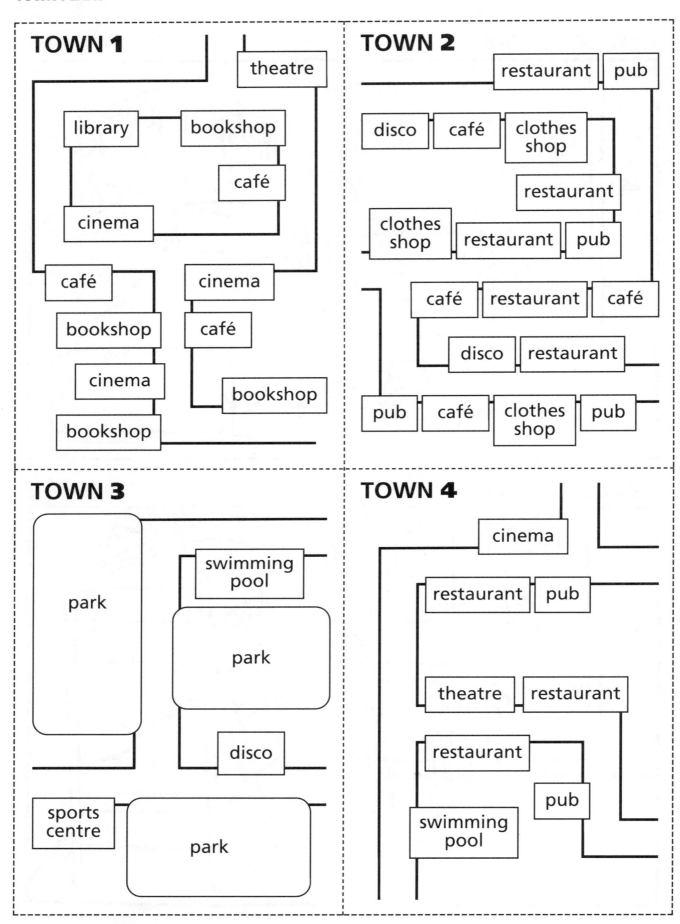

TOWN 1

theatre

library · bookshop

café

cinema

café · cinema

bookshop · café

cinema · bookshop

bookshop

TOWN 2

restaurant · pub

disco · café · clothes shop

restaurant

clothes shop · restaurant · pub

café · restaurant · café

disco · restaurant

pub · café · clothes shop · pub

TOWN 3

park

swimming pool

park

disco

sports centre · park

TOWN 4

cinema

restaurant · pub

theatre · restaurant

restaurant

pub

swimming pool

18 My home town (2)

QUESTIONNAIRE

(QUESTIONNAIRE)

What is important to you?
What do you want in the town where you live?

Libraries? ☐

Bookshops? ☐

Clothes shops? ☐

Pubs? ☐

Cafés? ☐

Restaurants? ☐

Swimming pools? ☐

Sports centres? ☐

Parks? ☐

Theatres? ☐

Cinemas? ☐

Discos? ☐

YOU CAN CHOOSE ONLY FIVE!

Mark them with a tick (✓)

19 Mother Hubbard (1)

CUPBOARD 1

SUGAR
250 grams

250 grams

Flour

BUTTER

100 grams

RECIPE 1

Shopping List

APPLE CAKE

500 grams flour

500 grams sugar

500 grams butter

8 eggs

6 apples

19 Mother Hubbard (2)

CUPBOARD 2

1 LITRE MILK

BUTTER

250 grams

RECIPE 2

CHEESE AND TOMATO OMELETTE

4 eggs

a little milk

100 grams cheese

4 tomatoes

Shopping List

20 Collectors

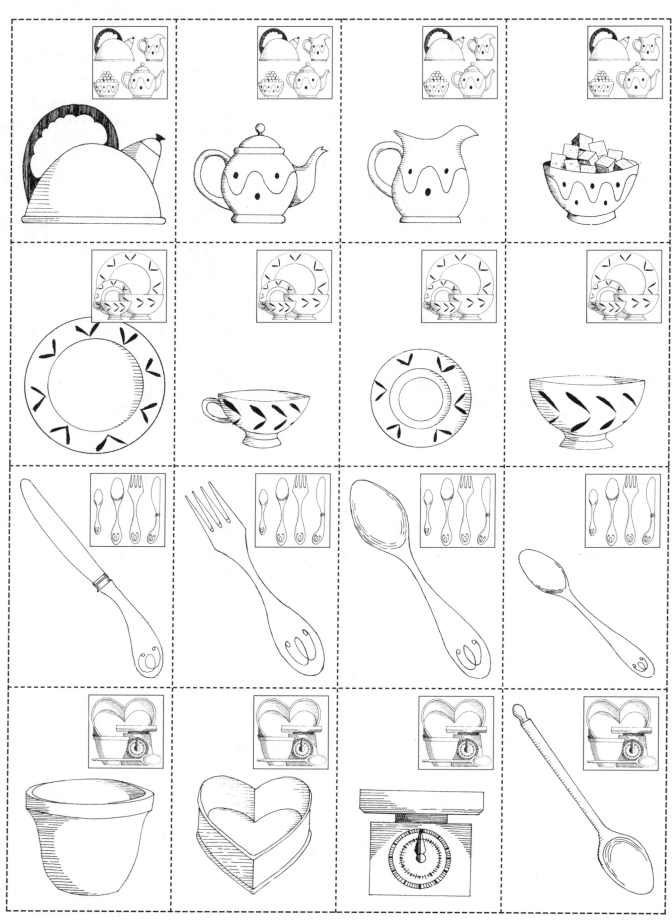

21 The great shopping race (1)

SHOP NAMES

SHOPPING LISTS

SHOPPING LIST		SHOPPING LIST		SHOPPING LIST	
200 grams	ham	6	rolls	1 bottle	aspirin
1 loaf	brown bread	1 bar	soap	1 jar	coffee
1 tube	toothpaste	1 packet	tea	6	bananas
500 grams	butter	4	oranges	1 box	chocolates
1 kilo	apples		car magazine	3	pork chops
1	evening newspaper	4	steaks	1	chocolate cake

SHOPPING LIST		SHOPPING LIST		SHOPPING LIST	
1 litre	milk	1 kilo	peas	1 packet	cigarettes
1 bag	potatoes	250 grams	sweets	500 grams	bacon
1 bar	chocolate	1 leg	lamb	1 loaf	white bread
1	chicken	5	jam tarts	1 bottle	deodorant
4	buns	1 bottle	shampoo	1 kilo	rice
1 box	plasters	500 grams	sugar	1	cauliflower

21 The great shopping race (2)
PRODUCT CARDS

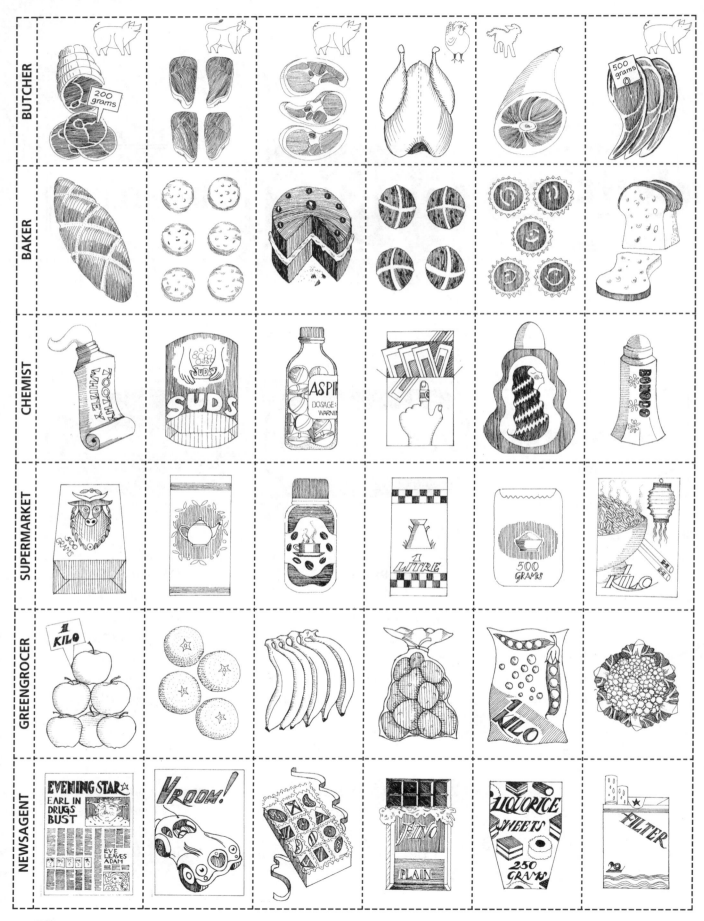

22 Martian lotto (1)

LOTTO BOARDS

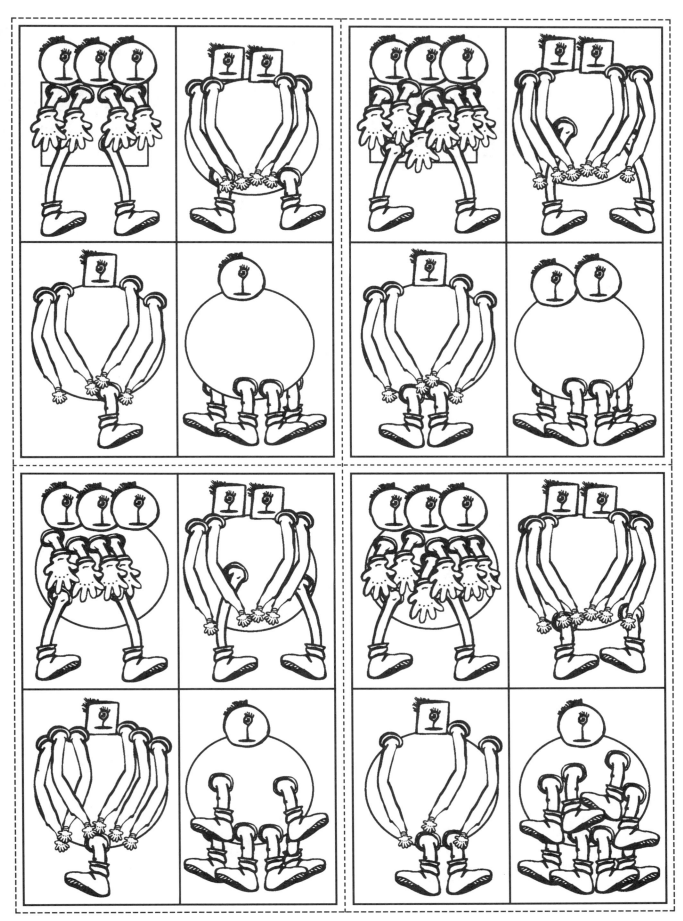

22 Martian lotto (2)

INDIVIDUAL CARDS

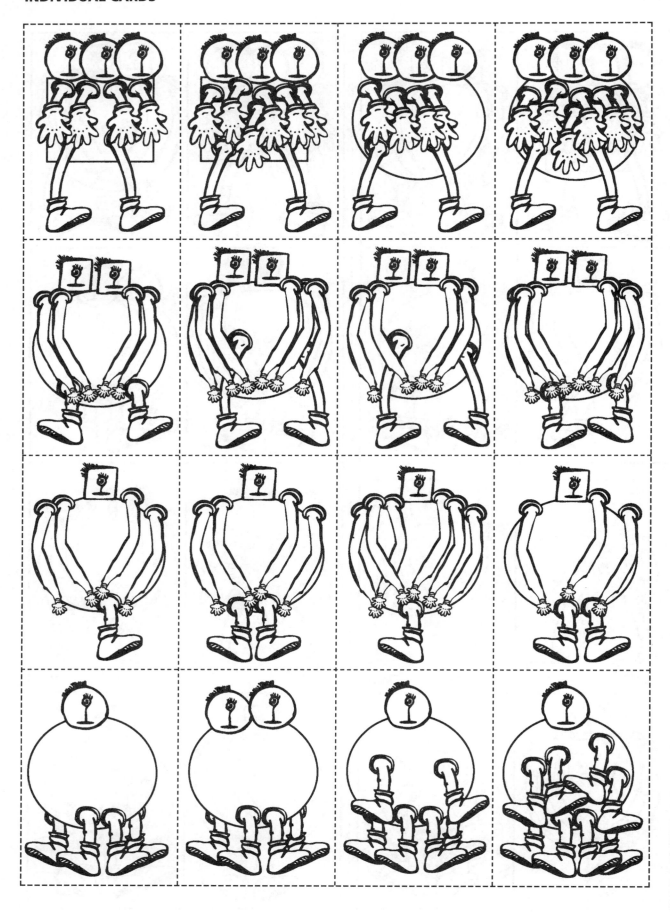

23 Airport convention (1)

MISSING PERSONS CARDS (1)

This is a photo of me. I will wear these clothes. See you soon!

This is a photo of me. I will wear these clothes. See you soon!

This is a photo of me. I will wear these clothes. See you soon!

This is a photo of me. I will wear these clothes. See you soon!

This is a photo of me. I will wear these clothes. See you soon!

This is a photo of me. I will wear these clothes. See you soon!

This is a photo of me. I will wear these clothes. See you soon!

This is a photo of me. I will wear these clothes. See you soon!

23 Airport convention (2)

MISSING PERSONS CARDS (2)

This is a photo of me. I will wear these clothes. See you soon!

This is a photo of me. I will wear these clothes. See you soon!

This is a photo of me. I will wear these clothes. See you soon!

This is a photo of me. I will wear these clothes. See you soon!

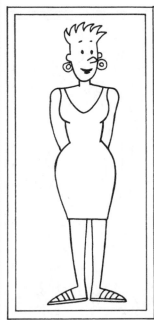

This is a photo of me. I will wear these clothes. See you soon!

This is a photo of me. I will wear these clothes. See you soon!

This is a photo of me. I will wear these clothes. See you soon!

This is a photo of me. I will wear these clothes. See you soon!

24 Follow the yellow brick road (1)

MAPS

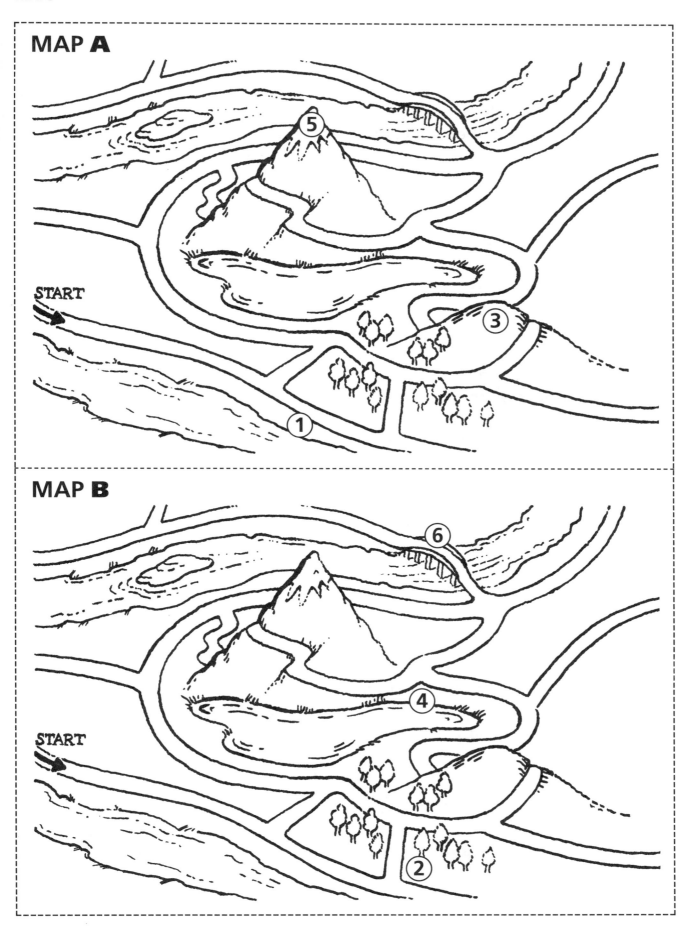

MAP **A**

START

MAP **B**

START

24 Follow the yellow brick road (2)

CLUE CARDS

1 Go along the road beside the river.
The next clue is on the river bank.

2 Go into the woods.
The next clue is in the middle of the woods.

3 Go up the hill.
The next clue is on top of the hill.

4 Go round the lake.
The next clue is beside the lake.

5 Go over the mountain.
The next clue is on top of the mountain.

6 Go across the bridge.
The last clue is on the bridge.

7 You are very near the treasure.
Write the names of the six places in the gaps:

1 ____ ____ ____ ____ ____   ____ ____ ____ ____

2 ____ ____ ____ ____ ____

3 ____ ____ ____ ____

4 ____ ____ ____ ____

5 ____ ____ ____ ____ ____ ____ ____ ____

6 ____ ____ ____ ____ ____ ____

8 Now take   the second letter of clue 1
the last letter of clue 2
the last letter of clue 3
the second letter of clue 4
the last letter of clue 5
the fourth letter of clue 6

Write the letters here to find the treasure.

The treasure is on the ____ ____ ____ ____ ____ ____ .

25 Dream tickets

HOBBY CARDS

YOU LIKE cycling.	YOU LIKE walking.	YOU LIKE skiing.	YOU LIKE painting.
YOU LIKE football.	YOU LIKE tennis.	YOU LIKE gardening.	YOU LIKE sailing.
YOU LIKE playing the guitar.	YOU LIKE cooking.	YOU LIKE riding.	YOU LIKE climbing.

HOLIDAY PRIZE CARDS

CONGRATULATIONS! • • • **YOU HAVE WON a cycling holiday in Switzerland**	**CONGRATULATIONS!** * * * YOU HAVE WON a week's Cordon Bleu cookery course	CONGRATULATIONS! • • • **YOU HAVE WON 4 tickets to the next World Cup final**	**CONGRATULATIONS!** * * * YOU HAVE WON a walking holiday in the Andes
CONGRATULATIONS! * * * YOU HAVE WON a painting course in The Netherlands	CONGRATULATIONS! • • • **YOU HAVE WON a week's skiing in Italy**	**CONGRATULATIONS!** * * * YOU HAVE WON a Gardens of England tour	CONGRATULATIONS! • • • **YOU HAVE WON a trip across the Atlantic in a sailing ship**
CONGRATULATIONS! • • • **YOU HAVE WON 2 tickets to next year's Wimbledon Tennis tournament**	**CONGRATULATIONS!** * * * YOU HAVE WON a place on an expedition to climb Mount Everest	CONGRATULATIONS! • • • **YOU HAVE WON a place on a camel ride across the Sahara**	**CONGRATULATIONS!** * * * YOU HAVE WON a week's guitar course in Spain

26 Lost tribes
TRIBE CARDS

You live in a straw house
beside the sea.

You eat fish.
You drink tea.
You like dancing.

You live in a mud house
in the country.

You eat rice.
You drink rice wine.
You like dancing.

You live in a wooden house
in the hills.

You eat corn.
You drink beer.
You like dancing.

You live in a tent
and move around.

You eat cheese.
You drink milk.
You like dancing.

27 Does it eat people?

NUMBER BOARD

1	2	3	4
5	6	7	8
9	10	11	12

ANIMAL BOARDS / CARDS

28 Jobmatch
JOB DESCRIPTION CARDS

get up 5 am
go to work 6 am
have lunch 11 am
come home 2 pm
go to bed 10 pm

POSTMAN

get up 5 am
go to work 5.30 am
have lunch 11 am
come home 7 pm
go to bed 10 pm

FARMER

get up 7.30 am
go to work 8.30 am
have lunch 12.30 pm
come home 4 pm
go to bed 11 pm

TEACHER

get up 8 am
go to work 2 pm
have lunch 12.30 pm
come home 10 pm
go to bed midnight

NURSE

get up 1 am, 3 am,
    4.15 am, 7.30 am
go to work 1.15 am,
    3.15 am, 4.30 am,
    7.45 am
have lunch 12 midday
come home 7.30 pm
go to bed 11 pm, 2 am,
    4 am, 5 am

DOCTOR

get up 3 pm
go to work 10 pm
have lunch 2 am
come home 6 am
go to bed 8 am

FACTORY WORKER

get up 1 pm
go to work 7 pm
have lunch 1.30 am
come home 4 am
go to bed 5 am

SINGER

get up 7.30 am
go to work 9 am
have lunch 1 pm
come home 5 pm
go to bed 11 pm

SECRETARY

29 World map (1)
WORLD MAP

WORLD MAP

29 World map (2)
PEOPLE CARDS

30 Lie detectors

ACTION CARDS

smile	cry	argue	do some exercise
tell a lie	read a book	clean the house	stay up all night
drive too fast	drink champagne	go to the cinema	spend too much money

FREQUENCY CARDS

Every day	Once a year	Never	Every night
Not very often	Once a week	On Monday mornings	At weekends
Once every five years	Twice a week	Often	Sometimes

31 Talent scouts

JOB BOARD / CARDS

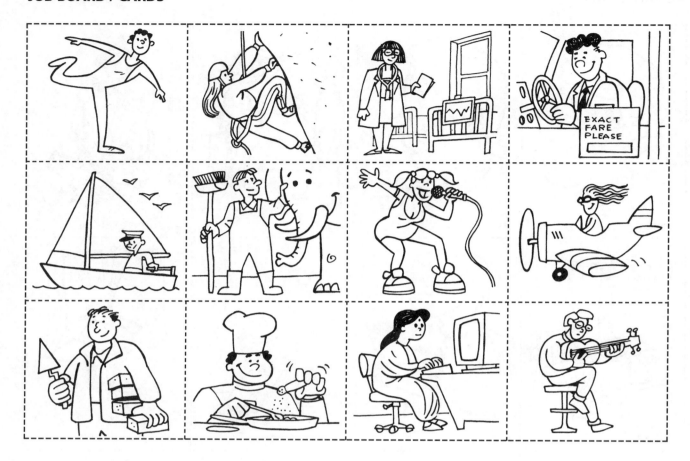

32 Room service (1)

SITUATION CARDS

32 Room service (2)

OBJECT CARDS

33 The restaurant game

MENU CARD

MENU

SOUP
tomato soup
chicken soup
vegetable soup
pea soup

STARTERS
prawn cocktail
avocado
grapefruit
melon

MAIN COURSES
fish and chips
sausage and beans
chicken pie and chips
cheese salad

DESSERTS
apple pie
chocolate pudding
ice cream
fruit salad

FOOD CARDS

34 Blind date

DIARIES

MON 21 *cinema????*

TUES 22

WED 23 AWAY

THURS 24 ON

FRI 25 HOLIDAY

SAT 26

SUN 27

MON 21 MEETING IN LONDON

TUES 22 disco ???

WED 23

THURS 24 AWAY

FRI 25 ON

SAT 26 HOLIDAY

SUN 27

MON 21 London

TUES 22

WED 23 swimming???

THURS 24

FRI 25 Away

SAT 26 on holiday

SUN 27

MON 21 London

TUES 22

WED 23

THURS 24 Party ???

FRI 25 Away on

SAT 26 holiday

SUN 27

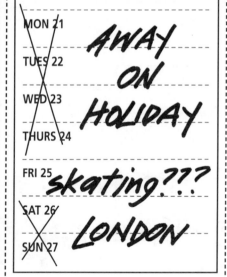

MON 21 AWAY

TUES 22 ON

WED 23 HOLIDAY

THURS 24

FRI 25 skating???

SAT 26 LONDON

SUN 27

MON 21

TUES 22 AWAY

WED 23 ON

THURS 24 HOLIDAY

FRI 25

SAT 26 theatre???

SUN 27 LONDON

MON 21

TUES 22 AWAY

WED 23 ON

THURS 24 HOLIDAY

FRI 25

SAT 26

SUN 27 picnic???

35 Noises off

ACTIVITY CARDS

36 Homelife
PICTURE BOARDS / CARDS

37 In the park

Park scene **A**

Park scene **B**

38 Eyewitnesses (1)

HOUSE PLAN

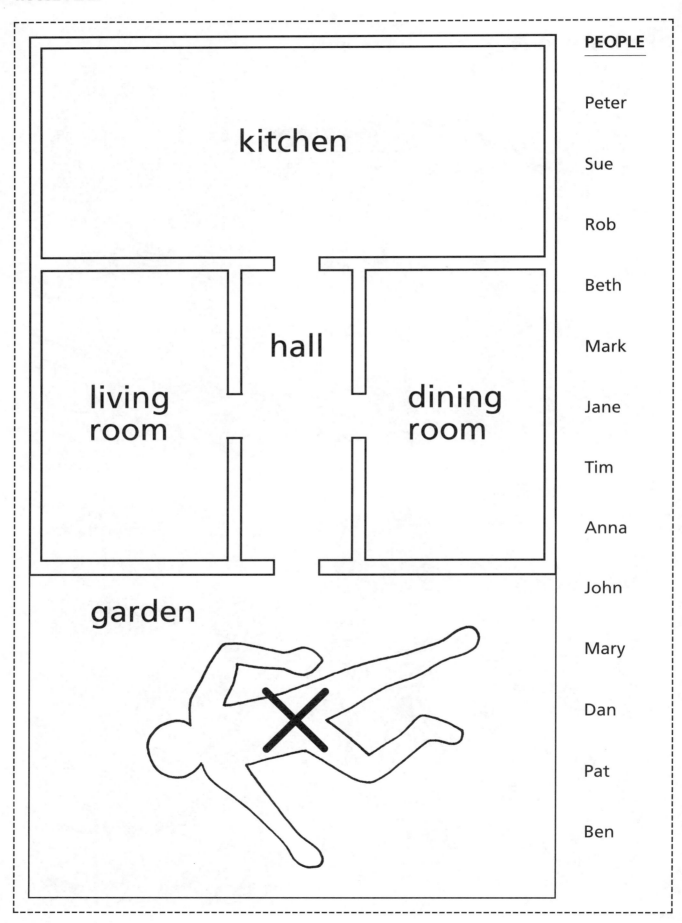

PEOPLE

Peter

Sue

Rob

Beth

Mark

Jane

Tim

Anna

John

Mary

Dan

Pat

Ben

38 Eyewitnesses (2)

ROLE CARDS

PETER
You were in the kitchen at 11 o'clock. SUE and ROB were with you.

SUE
You were in the kitchen at 11 o'clock. PETER and ROB were with you.

ROB
You were in the kitchen at 11 o'clock. SUE and PETER were with you.

BETH
You were in the living room at 11 o'clock. MARK and TIM were with you.

TIM
You were in the living room at 11 o'clock. BETH and MARK were with you.

MARK
You were in the living room at 11 o'clock. BETH and TIM were with you.

ANNA
You were in the dining room at 11 o'clock. JOHN and MARY were with you.

JOHN
You were in the dining room at 11 o'clock. ANNA and MARY were with you.

MARY
You were in the dining room at 11 o'clock. JOHN and ANNA were with you.

DAN
You were in the hall at 11 o'clock. BEN and PAT were with you.

BEN
You were in the hall at 11 o'clock. DAN and PAT were with you.

PAT
You were in the hall at 11 o'clock. BEN and DAN were with you.

POLICE OFFICER
You are here to find the murderer. Ask questions. Find out where everybody was at 11 o'clock.

39 Last night
ENTERTAINMENT CARDS

40 Souvenir shopping (1)

SOUVENIR CARDS

40 Souvenir shopping (2)
HOLIDAY SNAPS (1)

40 Souvenir shopping (3)
HOLIDAY SNAPS (2)

FRANCE

A fantastic castle

I thought I ordered salad not snails!

An amazing castle

GERMANY

Call this a HOLIDAY?

USA

Skyscrapers!

CHINA

A lovely temple

40 Souvenir shopping (4)
HOLIDAY SNAPS (3)

My favourite pagoda

JAPAN

A theatre

SWITZERLAND

After all that skiing we need a fondue!

I wish I had these in my garden — the tulips not the windmills!

THE NETHERLANDS

ENGLAND

The weather's cold but the beer's warm!

Beginners'
COMMUNICATION
Games

**RULES
SHEETS**

Rules sheets

Rules for Lotto Games 2, 3, 22 and 36

1 Take a board each.

2 Place the cards face down.

3 Player 1 takes the top card.

4 Don't show it to the others.

5 Tell the others about it.

6 The others ask questions.

7 The player with the matching picture takes the card.

8 Put it on the board.

9 The next player takes the top card.

10 The player who covers all the pictures first is the winner.

NOTES   For all games, make one copy of the strip cartoon. Make the following alterations for each game, then use this as your copymaster.

GAME 2	GAME 3	GAME 22	GAME 36
Delete Rule 6.	Delete Rule 6.	Rule 5: write 'He's got ... .' 'He hasn't got ... .' in the speech bubble.	Rule 5: write 'He/She/They' in the speech bubble.
Rule 5: delete 'about it' and add 'how to spell the word' to the rule.	Rule 5: delete 'it' and add 'the number of spots'. Then write 'Five spots' in the speech bubble.	Rule 6: write 'Has he got ...?' in the speech bubble.	Rule 6: write 'Is he/she ... -ing?' 'Are they ... -ing?' in the speech bubble.
Write 'C-A-T' in the speech bubble.			

106

Rules sheets

Rules for Lotto Game 7

1 Take a board each.

2 Place the cards face down.

3 Player 1 takes the top card.

4 Hold it up and ask, 'Whose is this?' or 'Whose are these?'

5 The player with the matching picture answers and takes the card.

6 Put it on the board.

7 The next player takes the next card.

8 The player who covers all the pictures first is the winner.

Rules for Quiz Game 29

1 One player is Quizmaster.

2 The others have a map each.

3 The Quizmaster has a pile of people cards.

4 He/She takes the top card.

5 Don't show it to the others.

6 The others ask questions.

7 The player who guesses the country keeps the card.

8 The player with the most cards at the end is the winner.

Rules sheets

Rules for Matching Games 30, 32 and 40

1 Deal out Pack 1.

2 Look at your cards.

3 Put Pack 2 face down.

4 Player 1 takes the top card.

5 Don't show it to the others.

6 Ask/Tell the others/one other person.

7 The player with the matching card replies/ chooses a card and replies.

8 If it's a good answer, throw away both matching cards.

9 The next player takes the top card.

10 The player with no cards is the winner.

NOTES   Make one copy of the strip cartoon. Make the following alterations for each game. Then use the copy as your copymaster.

GAME 30	GAME 32	GAME 40
Rule 6: delete 'Tell' and 'the others'. Write 'How often do you ...?' in the speech bubble.	Rule 6: delete 'Tell' and 'one other person'. Write 'Can I have ..., please?' in the speech bubble.	Rule 6: delete 'Ask' and 'one other person'. Write 'I saw ... .' 'I ate ... .' 'I drank ... .' 'I went ... .' in the speech bubble.
Rule 7: Delete 'with the matching card replies/' and write 'Every day' 'On Tuesdays, etc.' in the speech bubble.	Rule 7: delete 'chooses a card and replies' and write 'Certainly, sir/madam' in the speech bubble.	Rule 7: delete 'chooses a card and replies' and write 'Did you buy this there?' in the speech bubble.
	Rule 8: delete 'If it's a good answer.'	Rule 8: delete 'If it's a good answer.'

Rules sheets

Rules for Matching Games 4 and 14

1 Deal out Pack 1.

2 Look at your cards.

3 Put Pack 2 face down.

4 Player 1 takes the top card.

5 Don't show it to the others.

6 The others ask questions.

7 Player 1 answers.

8 Find the matching card.

9 Throw away both matching cards.

10 The next player takes the top card.

11 The player with no cards is the winner.

NOTES   Make one copy of the strip cartoon. Make the following alterations for each game. Then use this as your copymaster.

GAME 4	GAME 14
Rule 6: write 'What's the time?' in the speech bubble.	Rule 6: write 'What do you do?' in the speech bubble.
Rule 7: write 'It's ... .' in the speech bubble.	Rule 7: write 'I'm a ... .' in the speech bubble.

Rules sheets

Rules for Guessing Games 12 and 39

1 Spread out one pack of cards face up.

2 Put one pack of cards face down.

3 Player 1 takes the top card.

4 Don't show it to the others.

5 The others ask questions.

6 Player 1 answers.

7 The player who guesses can take the card(s).

8 She takes the top card.

9 The player with the most cards at the end is the winner.

NOTES Make one copy of the strip cartoon. Make the following alterations for each game. Then use this as your copymaster.

GAME 12	GAME 39
Rule 5: write 'Is it ...?' in the speech bubble.	Delete Rule 1.
Rule 6: write: 'Yes, it is/No, it isn't.' in the speech bubble.	Rule 5: write 'Did you ...?' in the speech bubble.
	Rule 6: write 'Yes, I did/No, I didn't.' in the speech bubble.

Rules sheets

Rules for Collecting Games 20 and 33

1 Read the menu.

2 Write down four things you want to eat (soup, starter, main course, dessert).

3 Don't show this to the others.

4 Deal out the cards.

5 Collect cards to make a set. Collect your four things to eat.

6 Player 1 asks any other player for a card.

7 If the player has the card, he MUST give it (if not, say 'Sorry!')

8 Then the next player asks.

9 The first player to collect a set of four cards is the winner.

NOTES   Make one copy of the strip cartoon. Make the following alterations for each game. Then use this as your copymaster.

GAME 20	**GAME 33**
Cut off the first three Rules. Renumber the remaining rules starting at 1.	Rule 5: delete 'Collect cards to make a set.'
Rule 5: delete 'Collect your four things to eat.'	Rules 6 and 8: write 'I'd like ... .' in the speech bubbles.
Rules 6 and 8: write 'Have you got ...?' in the speech bubbles.	Rule 7: write 'Certainly, sir/madam' in the speech bubble.
Picture 7: write 'Here you are!' in the speech bubble.	